CAMBRIDGE
UNIVERSITY PRESS

Psychology

for Cambridge International AS & A Level

WORKBOOK

Julia Russell, Lizzie Gauntlett & Amy Papaconstantinou

CAMBRIDGE
UNIVERSITY PRESS

University Printing House, Cambridge CB2 8BS, United Kingdom

One Liberty Plaza, 20th Floor, New York, NY 10006, USA

477 Williamstown Road, Port Melbourne, VIC 3207, Australia

314–321, 3rd Floor, Plot 3, Splendor Forum, Jasola District Centre, New Delhi – 110025, India

103 Penang Road, #05 -06/07, Visioncrest Commercial, Singapore 238467

Cambridge University Press is part of the University of Cambridge.

It furthers the University's mission by disseminating knowledge in the pursuit of education, learning and research at the highest international levels of excellence.

www.cambridge.org
Information on this title: www.cambridge.org/9781009152433

© Cambridge University Press 2022

First published 2016
Second edition 2022

20 19 18 17 16 15 14 13 12 11 10 9 8 7 6 5 4 3 2 1

Printed in Poland by Opolgraf

A catalogue record for this publication is available from the British Library

ISBN 978-1-009-15243-3 Workbook with Digital access

Additional resources for this publication at www.cambridge.org/delange
Cambridge University Press has no responsibility for the persistence or accuracy of URLs for external or third-party internet websites referred to in this publication, and does not guarantee that any content on such websites is, or will remain, accurate or appropriate. Third-party websites and resources referred to in this publication have not been endorsed by Cambridge Assessment International Education. Information regarding prices, travel timetables, and other factual information given in this work is correct at the time of first printing but Cambridge University Press does not guarantee the accuracy of such information thereafter.
Cover image: Hiroshi Watanabe/Getty Images

··

··

DEDICATED TEACHER AWARDS

Teachers play an important part in shaping futures. Our Dedicated Teacher Awards recognise the hard work that teachers put in every day.

Thank you to everyone who nominated this year; we have been inspired and moved by all of your stories. Well done to all of our nominees for your dedication to learning and for inspiring the next generation of thinkers, leaders and innovators.

Congratulations to our incredible winners!

WINNER

Regional Winner Middle East & North Africa	Regional Winner Europe	Regional Winner North & South America	Regional Winner Central & Southern Africa	Regional Winner Australia, New Zealand & South-East Asia	Regional Winner East & South Asia
Annamma Lucy GEMS Our Own English High School, Sharjah - Boys' Branch, UAE	**Anna Murray** British Council, France	**Melissa Crosby** Frankfort High School, USA	**Nonhlanhla Masina** African School for Excellence, South Africa	**Peggy Pesik** Sekolah Buin Batu, Indonesia	**Raminder Kaur Mac** Choithram School, India

For more information about our dedicated teachers and their stories, go to
dedicatedteacher.cambridge.org

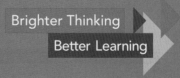

Building Brighter Futures **Together**

⟩ Contents

A Level

> Introduction

This workbook has been developed to support you as you study the Cambridge International AS & A Level Psychology syllabus (9990) for examination from 2024. The syllabus covers a range of approaches to the study of psychology including biological, cognitive, learning and social. At A Level you will apply your knowledge and understanding to important real-world issues in two of four options: clinical, consumer, health and organisational psychology. Research Methods are an essential part of psychology and underpin both AS and A Level Psychology.

The exercises in this resource will help you to apply what you have learned in different contexts. The chapters are arranged in the same order as the chapters in our Cambridge International AS & A Level Psychology coursebook. The first chapter contains 6 sub-sections that cover a wide variety of the research methods relevant to the syllabus.

The various features that you will find in these chapters are explained in the How to use this book section of this resource found on page viii.

> How to use this series

We offer a suite of resources for the Cambridge International AS & A Level Psychology syllabus. All of the books in the series work together to help students develop the necessary knowledge and skills required for this subject.

This coursebook provides full coverage of the Cambridge International AS & A Level Psychology syllabus (9990). Each chapter contains in-depth explanations of Psychology concepts with a variety of activities, classroom discussions and projects to keep students engaged. The application of research methods and issues and debates are highlighted in every topic through features. Each chapter ends with exam-style questions to help learners consolidate their understanding. Discussion points and activities promote active learning and assessment for learning.

This digital teacher's resource provides detailed guidance for teaching all of the topics of the syllabus. Common misconceptions are suggested, which identify the areas where students may need extra support, as well as an engaging bank of lesson ideas for each syllabus topic. Differentiation is also emphasised with advice on the identification of different learner needs and suggestions for appropriate interventions to support and stretch learners.

This workbook contains over 200 exercises, carefully constructed to help learners to develop the skills that they need to progress through their Psychology course, providing further practice for all of the topics in the coursebook. Learners encounter a variety of research methods throughout the course, and questions about these research methods appear at the end of each chapter for learners to practise applying their knowledge and understanding.

> How to use this book

Throughout this book, you will notice lots of different features that will help your learning.

LEARNING INTENTIONS

The learning intentions at the start of each chapter are taken from the coursebook and set the scene for each exercise, beginning with `In this exercise you will practice how to:', and indicate the important concepts. Some of these learning intentions are further supported in this workbook but may not be covered fully.

KEY WORDS

Definitions for chapter-related vocabulary are given at the start of exercises in Chapters 2–9. The definition of words in the margin are linked to the **exercises**, based on their relevance to the topic. You will also find definitions for these words in the glossary at the back of this book.

TIPS

The information in these boxes will offer support and guidance to help you get the most out of your study of AS & A Level Psychology.

Exercises

These help you to practise skills that are important for studying Cambridge International AS and A Level Psychology (9990).

Questions within exercises fall into one of three types:

Questions relating to the core study (AS Level) or area of psychology being studied (A Level). Note that this applies to Chapters 2–9; Chapter 1 considers specific Research methods and does not have Issues and Debates or Research Methods question boxes.

ISSUES AND DEBATES

These exercises will help you practise what you have learned about issues and debates.

RESEARCH METHODS

These exercises will help you practise what you have learned about research methods.

⟩ Chapter 1

Research methods

Experiments

Exercise 1

1   Harjit is conducting a laboratory study to investigate whether shy people and outgoing people differ in their cognition. She is using a maths test as a measure of cognitive processing.

   a   What is the independent variable in Harjit's study?

   b   What is the dependent variable in Harjit's study?

   c   i   How could Harjit use the maths test as a measure of cognitive processing?

   ii   Why is this a good way to measure the dependent variable?

   d   Which experimental design should Harjit use?

   e   State **one** strength of Harjit using an experiment as her research method.

2   Bo is planning a field experiment to investigate whether people are more likely to enjoy sport in the summer or the winter.

   a   How could Bo measure the variable of 'enjoyment of sport'?

   b   Bo knows he must control variables that could be important in his study.

   i   What variables should Bo control?

   ii   How could one of these variables be controlled?

   c   Bo cannot decide which experimental design to use.
   What experimental design should Bo use and why?

   d   Explain **one** weakness of using a field experiment as the research method in Bo's study.

Self-reports

Exercise 2

1 Tino wants to conduct an interview to find out which revision technique students believe leads to the best exam performance. She intends to interview students at different schools, each of which use at least two different revision techniques.

   a Tino wants to be able to ask the students questions that are relevant to them. However, not all of the schools use the same ways to revise.

      i   Which interview format should Tino choose?

      ii Suggest an open question and a closed question that Tino could ask about students' beliefs about revision techniques.

   b Tino's study could create ethical issues if the students' responses relate to certain members of staff at their school.

      How could Tino reduce potential harm to school staff?

   c Tino intends to use the students' exam result percentages to check their beliefs about the effectiveness of different techniques. She will analyse her results using only exam results for students preferring the three most common techniques and expects these to be watching videos, discussions and playing games. Tino will then summarise her data by calculating a measure of central tendency and the range of the students' exam results for each of the three chosen techniques.

      i   Which measure of central tendency should Tino use and why?

      ii Draw a table that Tino could use to display her summary data, based on her expectations.

2 Igor has conducted a study using a questionnaire to investigate how mothers and fathers differ in the way that they interact with their children.

   a Igor measured several variables. Two of these variables were:

      • play

      • helping.

      i   How could Igor have operationalised **one** of these variables?

      ii Why would it be good to **operationalise** the variable in this way?

   b Another of the variables that Igor measured was 'praise'. He measured this on a scale of 0 (no praise) to 10 (lots of praise) and calculated the average score for mothers and fathers.

      i   The table shows Igor's results. What should he write in the empty box?

	Mother	Father
	9.0	8.2

      ii Plot a bar chart of Igor's results.

> **KEY WORD**
>
> **operationalise:** to produce a clear definition or description of a variable so that it can be accurately manipulated, measured or quantified, and the study can be replicated. This includes the independent variable and dependent variable in experiments and the co-variables in correlations

Case studies

Exercise 3

1 Kalki has conducted a case study of a young boy who has a phobia of vehicles. She has collected a range of data about the types of vehicles that frighten him.

    a What other pieces of information about the boy's phobia could Kalki have collected in her case study?

    b Kalki collected qualitative data. Why was it good to collect this type of data in Kalki's study?

    c Kalki also collected quantitative data. This included the number of different coloured bikes, cars and vans he was afraid of.

        i Which measure of central tendency should Kalki use on this data?

        ii What type of graph should Kalki use for this data?

2 Colin is planning a case study about a company that makes wooden toys. The company has three workers, and their manager. Colin is interested in how they interact, cope with stress, motivate each other and make constructive criticisms of each other's work.

    a The main sample in Colin's study will be the three workers and their manager. What other people or sources of information could Colin use to collect data?

    b What techniques could Colin use in his case study and why?

    c Colin is aware that his study may raise ethical issues.

        i What ethical issues could arise in Colin's study?

        ii How could these ethical issues be resolved or minimised?

Observations

Exercise 4

1 Dr Lee is planning an observation of children in a park. She is investigating whether they prefer to play close to adults or away from adults, and is counting laughing and smiling to indicate preference. She has permission from her university and the park owners to hide cameras in trees in one part of a park. There is also a notice to parents at the park gate informing them that if they are willing for their children to participate in her study, they should go to one part of the park and if they are not willing, they should go a different part of the park (where there are no cameras).

    a i Is Dr Lee's observation overt or covert?

      ii Explain another feature of Dr Lee's observation.

      iii What is good about this feature of Dr Lee's observation?

    b Why it is necessary for Dr Lee to put the notice on the park gate?

2 Gathii conducted an observation. He collected data by pretending to be studying in a library. This enabled him to count how many male and female students came in and how long they spent there.

a   What ethical issue does Gathii raise by pretending to be studying?

b   Why would it matter if the students realised what Gathii was doing?

c   Which measure of central tendency should Gathii use on his data about the time male students spent in the library?

d   Draw a table for Gathii to use for a summary of his data.

Correlations

Exercise 5

1 Dani is concerned about her understanding of the results of her correlational study.

a   Explain to Dani what her results would show if the variables were:

   i   positively correlated

   ii   negatively correlated

b   Sketch **two** graphs to show Dani two different correlational relationships she could find.

c   Dani has heard the expression 'correlation does not mean causation' but does not understand it.

   Explain to Dani what the expression means.

2 Kimi asks each of his participants to tell him their favourite piece of music. As they listen to this music, he measures their pulse rate and the 'pace' of the music, that is, the speed of the rhythm. Kimi's aim is to find out whether there is a relationship between pulse rate and the pace of the music that is being listened to.

a   Identify the **two** co-variables in Kimi's study.

b   How could **one** of these variables be measured?

c   What would Kimi find if his results showed a negative correlation?

d   Kimi's friend Dani says that Kimi will not know whether it is the pace of the music, or the individual differences between participants who choose different types of music that is affecting their pulse.

   Explain why this is true and what alternative research method Kimi would have to use to solve this problem.

Longitudinal studies

Exercise 6

1 Izonebi is a teacher. She is planning an experiment with a longitudinal design. She is investigating which one of two new ways to learn during the second year of a psychology course is better for her students than her old way, which she used with her class during their first year. The two new learning methods are:

- self-testing
- online aids.

a What is Izonebi's independent variable?

b What controls could Izonebi use in her study?

c When should Izonebi test her students' ability?

d How could Izonebi test her students' ability?

2 Kofi is conducting a longitudinal study to investigate how prejudice changes with age. He collects yearly data from a self-report scale. This measures feelings of prejudice towards a named target on a scale of zero (not at all prejudiced) to 10 (very prejudiced).

a Is Kofi's data from this scale qualitative or quantitative?

b After 15 years, Kofi realises that views about prejudice have changed. Although his scale still measures consistently, it is no longer relevant to prejudice today.

  i Is this a problem of validity or reliability?

  ii Why might there be a disadvantage to changing the question to update it?

c Sketch and label the axes for a graph to show how Kofi could display his data.

Biological approach

In this chapter you will practise how to:

- describe and apply the concepts and terminology of the biological approach and its main assumptions

- explain and apply the psychology being investigated in the biological approach

- describe, evaluate and apply the three core studies from the biological approach

- apply relevant research methods to the biological approach

- consider issues and debates that are relevant to the biological approach.

Exercise 1 Assumptions of the biological approach

KEY WORD

rapid eye movement (REM) sleep: a stage of sleep in which our eyes move rapidly under the lids, which is associated with vivid, visual dreams

Each of the four approaches that you are studying has a set of underlying assumptions that guide the particular area of psychology and the research methods it uses. This exercise will enable you to demonstrate your understanding of the main assumptions of the biological approach.

Klara has two cats, Mimi and Ben. She is watching them **sleep**. Mimi is an 'outdoor' cat. He goes out into the garden whenever he likes, but Ben has always stayed indoors. As Mimi sleeps, Klara can see his eyes moving under his eyelids. She is imagining him having a **dream** about birds in the trees moving around and wonders what is making his eyes move. Ben's eyes are moving too, and she wonders what he could be dreaming about.

1   Outline one main assumption of the biological approach that is relevant to Klara's situation.

2   Explain why the assumption you have suggested in question 1 is relevant to Klara's situation.

KEY WORDS

sleep: a state of reduced conscious awareness and reduced movement that occurs on a daily cycle

dream: a vivid, visual sequence of imagery that occurs at regular intervals during sleep and is associated with rapid eye movements

2.1 Core study 1: Dement and Kleitman (sleep and dreams)

Exercise 2 The psychology being investigated

KEY WORDS

circadian rhythm: a cycle that repeats daily, i.e. approximately every 24 hours, such as the sleep/wake cycle

frequency: the number of events per fixed period of time, e.g. the number of eye movements per minute (approximately 60/minute in REM sleep) or the number of brain waves (cycles) per second or Hertz (Hz), e.g. 13–30 Hz for beta waves

ultradian rhythm: a cycle that repeats more often than daily, e.g. the occurrence of periods of dreaming every 90 minutes during sleep

---

This exercise will enable you to understand the psychology being investigated in the study by Dement and Kleitman.

Consider the observations about Bunim and his family below.

1   Explain the observations in terms of the psychology being investigated in the study by Dement and Kleitman. Try to use **at least one** of the key words in each answer. You can use the same key words more than once.

Observations about Bunim and his family	Explanation of Bunim's observations
a Bunim used to sleep regular hours, going to bed about 10.00 p.m. and waking up at about 7.00 a.m.	
b Bunim and his wife, Skylar, now have a baby. The baby's sleep rhythm has not settled down yet, she only sleeps for about three hours before waking up again.	
c Bunim can see the baby's eyes moving under her eyelids while she is asleep. Her eyes seem to move at a very constant rate. He wonders why.	

Exercise 3 Procedure

KEY WORD

non-rapid eye movement (nREM) sleep: the stages of sleep (1 to 4) in which our eyes are still. It is also called quiescent (quiet) sleep. It is not associated with dreaming

KEY WORDS

rapid eye movement (REM) sleep: a stage of sleep in which our eyes move rapidly under the lids, which is associated with vivid, visual dreams

quantitative data: numerical results about the amount or *quantity* of a psychological measure, such as pulse rate or a score on an intelligence test

qualitative data: descriptive, in-depth results indicating the *quality* of a psychological characteristic, such as responses to open questions in self-reports or case studies and detailed observations

This exercise will help you to demonstrate your knowledge of the procedure (including the research methods, experimental design, controls and techniques for data collection) used by Dement and Kleitman. Refer to Section 2.1 Core study 1 on Dement and Kleitman's study in the coursebook or the original research paper to check your answers.

1　Think about the research methods used in the study:

　a　Which research method was used to investigate a possible link between dream duration and the duration of **rapid eye movement (REM) sleep**?

　b　Which research method was used to investigate which stage of sleep dreams are usually reported from?

2　Think about where the study was conducted:

　a　Where were the participants tested in this study?

　b　Explain the choice of location.

3　Think about the variables that were measured:

　a　What **quantitative data** was collected in the study?

　b　What **qualitative data** was collected in the study?

4　Think about the techniques used to measure these variables:

　a　How were the participants' sleep patterns recorded in the study?

　b　Explain the choice of **one** of the techniques used in this study.

Make sure you are clear in your responses about the different studies that were conducted by Dement and Kleitman. Each one had a different aim, some different data collection techniques and different data analysis.

Exercise 4 Conclusions

The multiple choice questions that follow will help you to describe the conclusions of the study by Dement and Kleitman.

For each question, select either **one** or **two** options.

1   **One** conclusion relating to the findings of the study is that our sleep:

    A   includes an ultradian rhythm

    B   cannot be interrupted

    C   is improved by drinking caffeine

    D   is better if we do not dream.

2   **Two** conclusions from the findings of the study are that our dreams:

    A   are longer at the start of the night

    B   happen at 90-minute intervals

    C   are longer in the middle of the night

    D   have content that is related to our eye movements.

3   **Two** conclusions from the methods of study were that:

    A   the **electroencephalograph (EEG)** cannot estimate the time spent dreaming

    B   the **amplitude** of brain waves measured by the EEG increases steadily through the night

    C   the EEG gives an indication of where objects in our dreams are moving

    D   asking recently woken sleepers to estimate how long they have been asleep is not effective.

KEY WORDS

electroencephalograph (EEG): a machine used to detect and record electrical activity in the brain and muscles when many cells are active at the same time. It uses macro-electrodes, which are large electrodes stuck to the skin or scalp

amplitude: the 'height' of waves, e.g. on an EEG (indicating voltage)

2.2 Core study 2: Hassett et al. (monkey toy preferences)

Exercise 5 Main assumptions

> **KEY WORDS**
>
> **testosterone:** a hormone released mainly by the testes, so is considered to be a 'male' hormone. It is an example of an androgen
>
> **oestrogen:** a hormone released mainly by the ovaries, so is considered to be a 'female' hormone
>
> **socialisation:** the process of learning to behave in socially acceptable ways. This may differ somewhat for the two genders and in different cultures
>
> **gender stereotype:** a bias exhibited in society, which may be held by people and represented, for example, in books or toys that assign particular traits, behaviours, emotions, occupations, etc., to males and females

This exercise will help you to link the main assumptions of the biological approach to Hassett et al.'s study.

Hassett et al. investigated potentially biologically driven differences between young males and females.

1   Outline the main hormonal differences between young males and females.

2   These hormonal differences could affect brain development, both before and after birth.

    a   Describe **one** piece of evidence that suggests there are brain differences between males and females.

    b   As hormonal differences between the sexes begin to appear before birth, what must be controlling the development of these differences, and why?

3   Suggest **one** way that **play** might be the product of evolution, that is, have been important in helping early humans to survive.

> **KEY WORD**
>
> **play:** behaviour typical of childhood that appears to be done for fun rather than any useful purpose. It may be solitary or social and may or may not involve interaction with an object. Objects designed for the purpose of play are called 'toys'

Exercise 6 Procedure

This exercise will enable you to check your understanding of the procedure of Hassett et al.'s study.

1   Pick out the pairs of facts using the information in the box to answer the questions about the procedure of Hassett et al.'s study.

boys' toys	frequency	operational definitions
coders working together	girls' toys	plush
drag	hold	right
duration	left	wheeled

a   The monkeys' play with the toys was measured using

   i   .... and   ii   ....

b   The toys the monkeys played with were either

   i   .... or   ii   ....

c   The toys the children played with were classified as

   i   .... or   ii   ....

d   The monkeys' behaviours with the toys included

   i   .... and   ii   ....

e   Reliability was improved by using

   i   .... and   ii   ....

f   Toy position was counterbalanced by placing them alternately on the

   i   .... or   ii   ....

Exercise 7 Evaluation

This exercise will help you consider the strengths and weaknesses of different elements of the study.

1   Copy and complete the table, giving **one** strength or **one** weakness in relation to each point.

Aspect of the study by Hassett et al.		Description of one relevant strength or weakness
a	Analysing the rank of female monkeys	
b	Operational definitions used	
c	Ethical considerations of the study	

2   For **one** of the rows in the table in question 1, present an opposite viewpoint (for example, if you have described an ethical weakness, describe an ethical strength as well).

2.3 Core study 3: Hölzel et al. (mindfulness and brain scans)

Exercise 8 Mindfulness concepts

KEY WORD
mindfulness: a state achieved through meditation that aims to increase awareness of the present-moment experience and enable a person to look at themselves in a compassionate, non-judgemental way

This exercise will help you to check your understanding of the concepts used by Hölzel et al. in their study of a mindfulness-based stress reduction (MBSR) programme.

1   Match each concept to its correct description.

Concept relating to mindfulness	Description of concept
a sitting meditation	i guiding attention in a sequence through the head, torso, arms, legs etc., to achieve a perception of one's physical self as a complete whole.
b body scan	ii gentle stretching, slow movements and breathing exercises.
c mindfulness exercises	iii focusing on the sensation of breathing, then sounds, sights, tastes and other body sensations, as well as thoughts and emotions.
d mindful yoga	iv increasing awareness of the self and the current experience during activities such as walking, eating, taking a shower or washing the dishes.
e mindfulness in everyday life	v a range of activities to develop awareness of the present-moment and a compassionate, non-judgemental view of the self.

Exercise 9 Stress reduction programmes

This exercise will help you to understand how longitudinal studies and stress reduction programmes could be used.

Emily is a psychologist working in a large organisation that makes bottled drinks. She is responsible for staff welfare. Many members of staff are finding work stressful and the manager has made changes to working practices to improve the situation. The manager also wants Emily to help the employees. She is planning a study to compare the effectiveness of a new stress reduction programme that she has devised (Emily's Reduction of Stress Initiative or 'ERSI') with the MBSR programme used by Hölzel et al.

1   Emily will have two groups of employees, one to test each stress reduction programme.

   a   Explain why Emily needs to use two different groups rather than having one group of employees who experience one programme followed by the other.

   b   Suggest how Emily could decide which employees she uses for her study.

2   Emily needs to measure the effectiveness of the programmes.

   a   Describe how Emily could adapt **one** way that Hölzel et al. used to measure change in thinking and emotions to use in her study.

   b   The manager has also asked Emily to measure the stress of employees in relation to their work. Suggest **two** measures of stress that Emily could use that relate directly to working at the bottled drinks company.

Exercise 10 Findings

The multiple choice questions that follow will help you to describe the findings of the study by Hölzel et al.

For each question, select **one** option.

1 The results suggest that in terms of **localisation of function**, **one** important area for the effects of MBSR is:

  A the posterior cerebellum

  B the hypothalamus

  C the lateral cerebellum

  D the insula.

2 **Two** conclusions from the study were that:

  A areas relating to the brain functions of learning and memory are affected by MBSR

  B areas relating to the brain functions of emotions and cognition are not affected by MBSR

  C structural changes in the brain can happen within an eight-week period

  D increases in grey matter concentration in the right temporo-parietal junction are important

> **KEY WORD**
>
> **localisation of function:** the way that particular brain areas are responsible for different activities

RESEARCH METHODS

This exercise considers the methods and procedures of each of the three core studies from the biological approach. It will help you to describe and compare the studies.

1 Using the information in the following grid, find the four boxes that belong to each of the three core studies. Use the row headings in the table below to help you.

A It included an experiment which compared the same group of people twice.	B It included an experimental comparison between two different groups of participants.	C It included an experiment and a correlation.
D Participants were tested in a laboratory-type setting and were attached to a piece of equipment.	E The main participants were not tested in a laboratory setting.	F Participants were tested in a laboratory-type setting and were put inside a piece of equipment.
G Participants were not given an interview or a questionnaire.	H Participants were given a questionnaire.	I Some participants were interviewed.

CONTINUED

J Some aspects of the participants' prior experiences were known.	K Some aspects of the participants' prior experiences were controlled for.	L Many aspects of the participants' present and prior experiences were controlled.

	Dement and Kleitman	Hassett et al.	Hölzel et al.
a Research method	i	ii	iii
b Setting	i	ii	iii
c Data collection technique	i	ii	iii
d Information about participants	i	ii	iii

2   Provide an additional detail relating to controls for each study in the bottom line of the table.

ISSUES AND DEBATES

This exercise will enable you to consider the issues and debates relevant to Dement and Kleitman's study. It will also enable you to check your understanding of how to evaluate the study in terms of its strengths and weaknesses.

1   Copy and complete the table. Name the issue or debate that is most relevant to each statement below about Dement and Kleitman's study. Describe **one** way in which each statement relates to the issue or debate you have named.

Statement about the study	Relevant issue/debate	How the issue/debate relates to the statement about the study
a Research following Dement and Kleitman's study found that people's dreams can be linked to noises they hear when sleeping.	i	ii

KEY WORD

correlation coefficient: a number between −1 and 1 that shows the strength of a relationship between two variables, with a coefficient of −1 meaning there is a perfect negative correlation and a coefficient of 1 meaning there is a perfect positive correlation

CONTINUE

Statement about the study	Relevant issue/debate	How the issue/debate relates to the statement about the study
b One question is whether children's dream experience is similar to adults' but Dement and Kleitman did not test this.	i	ii
c Studies before Dement and Kleitman's used animals such as cats to understand sleep and to test the techniques they used.	i	ii
d To help patients with sleep problems it is often important to know what stage of sleep they are in.	i	ii

2   For each of the statements in question 1, consider whether you could link the statement to the 'other' side of the issue or debate you have described in your answer.

3   Considering all the statements and your answers, analyse the extent to which the findings of the study are generalisable.

› Chapter 3
Cognitive approach

In this chapter, you will practise how to:

- describe and apply the concepts and terminology of the cognitive approach and its main assumptions

- explain and apply the psychology being investigated in the cognitive approach

- describe, evaluate and apply the three core studies from the cognitive approach

- apply relevant research methods to the cognitive approach

- consider issues and debates that are relevant to the cognitive approach.

Exercise 1 Assumptions of the cognitive approach

KEY WORDS

processing: how information is dealt with, for example thinking and decision-making in the brain and brain functions such as short-term and long-term memory

output: how we send information out, for example voice and body (such as hands for writing, drawing, moving)

Each of the four approaches that you are studying has a set of underlying assumptions that guide the area of psychology that is studied and the research methods used. This exercise will enable you to demonstrate your understanding of the main assumptions of the cognitive approach.

Charlie and Samia are riding their new bikes. Charlie's mum notices that they are both having problems. She wonders if this is because Charlie never looks where he is going. He seems to be clumsy even when he is walking. Charlie's dad suggests that Samia might find it easier because she listens to instructions better. Samia's aunt is watching the children. She says that all children need to pay attention to the way that the world moves past as the bike goes forwards and how the pedals feel as you push. She watches both children falling off and says this is a good thing as they must understand what effect their pedalling and steering has on the bike.

1   Suggest **one** main assumption of the cognitive approach that is relevant to children's progress with their bikes.

2   Apply this assumption to the situation described above.

TIP

Make sure you are clear in your responses about which assumption you are referring to. One is about differences (and similarities) between *different* people, the other is about similarities (and differences) between *computers* and people.

3.1 Core study 1: Andrade (doodling)

Exercise 2 Procedure

KEY WORD

dependent variable: the factor in an experiment that is measured and is expected to change under the influence of the independent variable

---

These questions will help you to demonstrate your knowledge of the procedure (including the research methods, experimental design, controls and research techniques for data collection) used by Andrade. Refer to Section 3.1 Core study 1 on Andrade's study in the coursebook or the original research paper to check your answers.

1   Think about when and where the study was conducted.

    a   Why was the timing of the participants' recruitment important in this study?

    b   Thinking about where the study was conducted, what type of experiment was this and why?

2   Think about the variable that was being manipulated in this study.

    a   What was the variable being manipulated?

    b   How were two conditions achieved in this study?

3   Think about the variables that were being measured in this study.

    a   What data was collected in the study?

    b   What was the data measuring?

4   Think about the **controls** in this study.

    a   What control measures were used?

    b   Why were these controls used?

KEY WORD

controls: ways to keep potential confounding variables constant, e.g. between levels of the independent variable, to ensure measured differences in the dependent variable are likely to be due to the independent variable, raising validity

---

TIP

The way you think about the procedure of each core study is important not just to help you understand all the essential parts of the study itself but also to ensure you are familiar with these central ideas for each type of research method. This understanding will help you to plan new studies.

Exercise 3 Results and conclusion

KEY WORDS

subjectivity: the effect of an individual's personal viewpoint on, for example, how they interpret data. Interpretation can differ between individual researchers as a viewpoint may be biased by one's feelings, beliefs or experiences, so is not independent of the situation

arousal: the extent to which we are alert, for example responsive to external sensory stimuli. It has physiological and psychological components and is mediated by the nervous system and hormones

This exercise will help you to show your understanding of how the findings of the study by Andrade, and the research methods relevant to the cognitive approach, could be applied.

Girvan has been told off by his teacher for doodling. He decides to do a **case study** on himself to see when he doodles, what he doodles and how well he remembers the lesson.

1 Why might Girvan's teacher be wrong to tell Girvan off?

2 Explain what Girvan should discover about how well he remembers the lesson in relation to his doodling.

3 Suggest why Girvan's results could be biased.

KEY WORD

case study: a research method in which a single instance, e.g. one person, family or institution, is studied in detail

TIP

Some questions start with a story (scenario). Make sure you apply your answers to the scenario when appropriate. This means more than just using any names given in the scenario. You need to relate the ideas or points you are making in your answer directly to the information you have been given in the scenario.

Exercise 4 The psychology being investigated

KEY WORDS

dual task situation: an experimental set-up that includes simultaneous cognitive demands of a primary task and a concurrent task.

concurrent task: an additional activity with a cognitive demand that we can perform at the same time as a main (primary) task

primary task: the activity we are supposed to be concentrating on, even though we may be doing something else as well, such as doodling

This exercise will help you to show your understanding of the psychology that was investigated by Andrade.

1   Dillon is conducting a study about student behaviours that could help them to concentrate. However, he has told the participants that the study is about student time-wasting. He is testing two groups of participants who have been instructed to engage in two different tasks, doodling and pen chewing. The participants believe these are time-wasting tasks, but Dillon has chosen them as activities which may prevent daydreaming.

Complete the paragraph about Dillon's study. Fill in the gaps using words or phrases from the box.

> attend   concurrent   daydreaming   debrief
> **dual task situation**   primary   time-wasting task

a   Dillon has two groups of participants and asks each group to perform one of the activities he calls 'time-wasting tasks'. They do this while they listen to a recorded lecture, which is the main source of information of the **input** that needs to be focused on, that is, to which they need to **i** ....
As the participants are expected to perform two activities at the same time, this is a **ii** .... Listening to the lecture is the **iv** .... cognitive task and the activity of either doodling or pen-chewing is the **v** .... cognitive task. After the lecture, Dillon will measure how much the participants can remember from the lecture. He hopes that one of the activities will have reduced **vi** .... , in which case the participants' recall of the lecture will be better. Finally, Dillon must **vii** .... his participants as he has deceived them by telling them that the task they were performing in addition to the lecture was a **viii** ....

b   Explain why it is important that Dillon excludes any participants in the doodling group who chew their pens.

> **KEY WORD**
>
> **input:** how we take incoming information in, for example eyes (detecting light, colour and movement), ears (detecting sound) and skin (detecting pressure)

3.2 Core study 2: Baron-Cohen et al. (Eyes test)

Exercise 5 Background

KEY WORD
ceiling effect: this occurs when a test is too easy and all participants in a condition achieve a very high score. This is problematic as it does not allow the researcher to differentiate between results

The aim of the study by Baron-Cohen et al. was to investigate the effectiveness of a revised version of the 'Reading the Mind in the Eyes' Test (Eyes test) compared with the original version of the Eyes test. To be able to show your understanding of this aim you will need to be confident about how the two versions of the test were different. This exercise will help you to show your understanding of the background to the study by Baron-Cohen et al.

1   Copy and complete the table below.

    a   Describe **three** features in the original version of the Eyes test.

    b   Describe how the features were different in the revised version of the Eyes test.

    c   For each comparison in the table, explain the problem with the original version of the Eyes test and why the change in the revised version of the Eyes test was better.

a Feature in the original version of the Eyes test	b Feature in the revised version of the Eyes test	c Why the feature was problematic in the original version and how the improved version overcame this problem
i	i	i
ii	ii	ii
iii	iii	iii

Exercise 6 Results and conclusion

Questions like the ones in this exercise will help you to demonstrate your knowledge of the results of the study (including the type of data, how the data were or could have been analysed, how the data were or could have been displayed and what they show, that is, what can be concluded from the results). Refer to Section 3.2 Core study 2 on Baron-Cohen et al.'s study (Eyes test) in the coursebook or the original research paper to check your answers.

Data

1 **a** Were the results of the study qualitative or quantitative?

b Was the data on gender recognition collected using an open or a closed question?

Analysis

2 **a** Which **measure of central tendency** was used to analyse the results of the Eyes test?

b Could a different measure of central tendency have been used? Explain your answer.

c Which **measure of spread** was used to analyse the results of the Eyes test?

d Could a different measure of spread have been used? Explain your answer.

e What graph(s) were or could have been used to display the Eyes test results?

Conclusion

3 **a** What can be concluded from the results of this study?

b Analyse the results of this study in terms of **generalisability**.

> **KEY WORDS**
>
> **measure of central tendency:** a mathematical way to find the typical or average score from a data set, using the mode, median or mean
>
> **measure of spread:** a mathematical way to describe the variation or dispersion within a data set
>
> **generalisability:** how widely findings apply, e.g. to other settings and populations

> **TIP**
>
> When thinking about the results of a study, remember to consider not only what the results show but also what they do not show. Think about whether there are questions that the results leave unanswered and what else would need to be done to answer those questions.

Exercise 7 Ethical issues

> **KEY WORDS**
>
> **autism spectrum disorder (ASD):** a diagnostic category (previously including Autism and Asperger's syndrome). Symptoms, appearing in childhood, present a range of difficulties with social interaction and communication and restricted, repetitive or inflexible behaviours or interests
>
> **informed consent:** knowing enough about a study to decide whether you want to agree to participate
>
> **protection from harm:** participants should not be exposed to any greater physical or psychological risk than they would expect in their day-to-day life
>
> **right to withdraw:** a participant should know they can remove themselves, and their data, from a study at any time

This exercise will enable you to consider the ethical issues and guidelines relevant to Baron-Cohen et al.'s study. It will also allow you to evaluate the study in terms of its ethical strengths and weaknesses.

1 Copy and complete the table. For each feature of the study (**a–e**):

   i State the ethical issue identified in the feature of the study described.

   ii Name a relevant ethical guideline that either could have been broken or was followed in this study.

   iii Describe whether each ethical guideline was broken or followed in the study by Baron-Cohen et al.

Feature of the study	Ethical issue	Ethical guideline	How the ethical guideline was broken or followed
a Some people with **autism spectrum disorder** avoid eye-contact with others.	i	ii	iii
b Some of the words and definitions were of unpleasant emotions such as accusing, alarmed, hateful, terrified.	i	ii	iii
c The researchers measured some participants' IQ scores.	i	ii	iii
d Participants knew what they would be assessed for.	i	ii	iii

2 For each ethical guideline you have identified as broken in question 1, explain why this feature was necessary to achieve valid results.

3.3 Core study 3: Pozzulo et al. (line ups)

Exercise 8 Aims

This exercise will help you to show your understanding of the aim of the study by Pozzulo et al.

1   Match the terms used in the core study with their correct definitions.

Terms		Definition	
a	identification	**i**	an array of faces that does not include the target face or culprit of a crime
b	rejection	**ii**	an array of faces that includes the target face or culprit of a crime
c	target-absent line-up	**iii**	correctly saying a face is not in an array of faces, or selecting a 'blank silhouette', when a target face is not present
d	target-present line-up	**iv**	correctly selecting a target face when it is present in an array of faces

2   Complete the sentences below about Pozzulo et al.'s study. Fill in the gaps using words from the box.

absent   cognitive   present   social

    a   The aim of the study by Pozzulo et al. was to test the prediction that children

        responded with more 'false positives' in target-**i** ....

        line-ups than in target-**ii** .... line-ups.

    b   This was because the choice in the former situation was driven more by

        i .... factors than by **ii** .... factors.

Exercise 9 Procedure

This exercise will help you to show your understanding of the procedure of the study by Pozzulo et al.

1 Four predictions were tested in the study. They were:

I Children will be as good as adults at identifying cartoon faces in line-ups.

II Children will be worse than adults at identifying human faces in line-ups.

III Children will be worse than adults at rejecting cartoon faces in line-ups.

IV Children will be worse than adults at rejecting human faces in line-ups.

Identify which of these predictions (I–IV) were tested in the following procedures:

a Comparison of children and adults with Dora and Diego in target-absent line-ups.

b Comparison of children and adults with pictures of people's faces in target-present line-ups.

c Comparison of children and adults with pictures of people's faces in target-absent line-ups.

d Comparison of children and adults with Dora and Diego in target-present line-ups.

2 The statements below describe the procedure of the study for the child participants. Some parts of the procedure were repeated for different conditions – you do not have to include these repeats. Put the steps into the correct order.

A The children were shown line-up photos.

B The children were shown a video.

C The experimenters did craft work with the children.

D The children were told to pay attention.

E The children were asked a **filler question**.

> **KEY WORD**
>
> **filler questions:** items put into a questionnaire, interview or test to disguise the aim of the study by hiding the important questions among irrelevant ones so that participants are less likely to work out the aims and then alter their behaviour

Exercise 10 Evaluation

> **KEY WORDS**
>
> **reliability:** the extent to which a procedure, task or measure is consistent, for example, that it would produce the same results with the same people on each occasion
>
> **sample:** the group of people selected to represent the population in a study
>
> **validity:** the extent to which the researcher is testing what they claim to be testing
>
> **independent measures:** an experimental design in which a different group of participants is used for each level of the independent variable (condition)
>
> **Interview:** a research method using verbal questions asked directly, using techniques such as face-to-face or telephone
>
> **questionnaire:** a self-report research method that uses written questions, through a 'paper and pencil' or online technique

This exercise will help you to consider the strengths and weaknesses of the study by Pozzulo et al.

1   For each issue in the table, think of an evaluation point for the study by Pozzulo et al. and state whether it is a strength or a weakness. Try to include at least one of each.

For each issue, explain your evaluation point.

Issue	Strength or weakness?	Explanation of evaluation point
a Reliability	i	ii
b Validity	i	ii
c Sample	i	ii
d Ethics	i	ii

RESEARCH METHODS

This exercise will enable you to describe the methodology used in studies from the cognitive approach.

1   Describe how each term relates to the example of the study given.

Term	Example of study	Description
a Control condition	Andrade	
b Experimental condition	Pozzulo et al.	
c Interview	Pozzulo et al.	
d Questionnaire	Baron-Cohen et al.	
e Repeated measures	Pozzulo et al.	
f Independent measures	Baron-Cohen et al.	
g Counterbalancing	Andrade	

2   Deming is planning an experiment to explore male and female students' views about being tested by continuous assessment or exams. Two of Deming's friends are helping him to choose which self-report method to use to collect data. Simeon says he should use written questions, whereas Rania suggests using verbal questions. Deming asks his friends what his experimental design will be as he will have a different group of participants for each level of the **independent variable**.

Identify the parts of the paragraph about Deming's experiment that relate to each of these terms:

independent measures

independent variable

interview

questionnaire.

KEY WORD

independent variable: the factor under investigation in an experiment that is manipulated to create two or more conditions (levels) and is expected to be responsible for changes in the dependent variable

ISSUES AND DEBATES

This exercise will help you to reflect on how the studies in the cognitive approach relate to one of the psychological issues and debates considered at AS Level.

1 Copy and complete the table. Use evidence from each core study to support either viewpoint in the debate about the use of children in psychology. Make at least one comment on each side of the table for each of the studies.

Core study	Children cannot or should not be used in such research	Children can or should be used in such research
a Andrade (doodling)	i	ii
b Baron-Cohen et al. (Eyes test)	i	ii
c Pozzolo et al. (line–ups)	i	ii

KEY WORDS

protection from harm: participants should not be exposed to any greater physical or psychological risk than they would expect in their day-to-day life

autism spectrum disorder (ASD): a diagnostic category (previously including Autism and Asperger's syndrome). Symptoms, appearing in childhood, present a range of difficulties with social interaction and communication and restricted, repetitive or inflexible behaviours or interests

social desirability bias: trying to present oneself in the best light by determining what a task requires

TIP

To explore some debates in full, such as the ones relating to children and animals in research, you must be able to consider examples of research that *have* used children or animals as well as examples of whether and how children or animals *could be used* in other research. In this case, it means that you need to consider the use of children in the study by Pozzolo et al. as well as whether or how children could be used in studies such as those conducted by Andrade and Baron-Cohen et al.

> Chapter 4

Learning approach

LEARNING INTENTIONS

In this chapter you will practise how to:

- describe and apply the concepts and terminology of the learning approach and its main assumptions

- explain and apply the psychology being investigated in the learning approach

- describe, evaluate and apply the three core studies from the learning approach

- apply relevant research methods to the learning approach

- consider issues and debates that are relevant to the learning approach.

Exercise 1 Assumptions of the learning approach

KEY WORDS

operant conditioning: learning through the consequences of our actions

stimulus: an event or object that leads to a behavioural response

blank slate: the idea that all individuals are born without any mental content, and that all knowledge must come from experience

phobia: the irrational, persistent fear of an object or event (stimulus) that poses little real danger but creates anxiety and avoidance in the sufferer

Each of the four approaches that you are studying has a set of underlying assumptions that guide the particular area of psychology and the research methods it uses. This exercise will enable you to demonstrate your understanding of the main assumptions of the learning approach.

1 Complete the following sentences about the assumptions of the approach, filling in the gaps using the words from the box.

| response | social | experiences | blank slate | classical |

a Each life begins as a **i** '.....................................': observable changes to our behaviour result from **ii** .... and interaction with our environments.

b The processes of i .... learning, **operant conditioning** and

ii .... conditioning are the ways in which humans and

animals learn via the **stimulus–iii** _____ model.

2 Choose one of the assumptions of the learning approach. Explain how the assumption can be applied to each of the following studies:

a Bandura et al. (aggression)

b Fagen et al. (elephant learning)

c Saavedra and Silverman (button **phobia**)

4.1 Core study 1: Bandura et al. (aggression)

Exercise 2 The psychology being investigated

This exercise will enable you to show your understanding of the psychology that Bandura et al. investigated.

Damon wants to encourage his children to show less **aggression** when they are playing together. He plans to give his children chocolate at the end of the week as a reward for not playing aggressively. Damon's friend suggests it might be more effective for Damon to show his children how to play calmly without being aggressive.

1 Explain why showing children how to play calmly might be more effective than giving them chocolate for not being aggressive. Refer to **social learning theory** in your answer.

2 State both forms of learning Damon could use.

Exercise 3 Results

In this exercise, you will consider the results of the study.

1 Outline **one** difference in non-aggressive play between boys and girls.

2 Describe **one** finding about imitative physical aggression from the study.

3 Describe **one** finding about the influence of a same-sex **model** from the study.

> **KEY WORDS**
>
> **aggression:** behaviour that is aimed at harming others either physically or psychologically
>
> **social learning theory:** the learning of a new behaviour that is observed in a role model and imitated later in the absence of that mode.

> **KEY WORD**
>
> **model:** a person who inspires or encourages others to imitate positive or negative behaviours

> **TIP**
>
> There were three independent variables (IVs) in the study by Bandura et al. (model type, child gender, model gender) and the dependent variable (DV) was the learning of the children. When reporting findings, ensure you indicate the effect of the IV (including level) on the DV.

Exercise 4 Ethical issues

KEY WORDS

validity: the extent to which the researcher is testing what they claim to be testing

reliability: the extent to which a procedure, task or measure is consistent, for example, that it would produce the same results with the same people on each occasion

This exercise will help you to consider the ethical guidelines and issues relevant to Bandura et al. It will also allow you to evaluate the study in terms of its ethical strengths and weaknesses.

KEY WORD

ethical issues: problems in research that raise concerns about the welfare of participants (or have the potential for a wider negative impact on society)

1 Copy and complete the table. For each feature of the study, identify a relevant ethical guideline that either could have been broken or followed in the study and describe why each feature was or was not an **ethical issue**.

Feature of the study	Ethical issue	Ethical guideline
a Participants were shown aggressive behaviour and speech during the study.	i	ii
b The study involved young children.	i	ii
c It is not clear whether parents knew their children were part of the study.	i	ii
d Participants were frustrated by being told not to play with certain toys.	i	ii

2 For each ethical guideline you have identified as broken in question 1, explain why this feature was necessary to achieve valid results.

TIP

Ethical guidelines and ethical issues are related but are two distinct ideas in psychology. The guidelines are the rules that psychologists must follow (for example, 'protection from harm'), whereas an ethical issue occurs within a particular piece of research when psychologists must consider if/how a guideline can be followed (for example, if the study might distress the participants).

4.2 Core study 2: Fagen et al. (elephant learning)

Exercise 5 Aims

In this exercise you will consider the aim of the study, including the relevant key concepts.

The aim of the study by Fagen et al. was to investigate whether free-contact, traditionally trained elephants can be trained to participate in a trunk wash by using positive reinforcement.

1   Copy and complete the table with definitions of the key concepts.

Key concepts	Definition
a free-contact, traditionally trained	
b trunk wash	
c positive reinforcement	

Exercise 6 Conclusions

This exercise will help you to consider the conclusions of the study by Fagen et al.

1   State the conclusion of the study by Fagen et al.

2   Outline an example from the findings of the study that supports the conclusion.

3   Explain the usefulness of the study by Fagen et al. to the real world.

Exercise 7 Evaluation

KEY WORD

sample: the group of people selected to represent the population in a study

This exercise will help you consider the strengths and weaknesses of different elements of the study.

1 Consider each evaluative issue in the table. Explain how each issue was a strength of the study, a weakness of the study, or both.

Issue	Strength/Weakness?	Explanation
a Replicability	i	ii
b Reliability	i	ii
c Validity	i	ii
d Sample	i	ii
e Ethical Issues	i	ii

4.3 Core study 3: Saavedra and Silverman (button phobia)

Exercise 8 Background

KEY WORD

classical conditioning: learning through association, studied in both humans and animals

This exercise will help you to demonstrate your understanding of the psychology investigated by Saavedra and Silverman.

Simone has a strong dislike of apples. Simone's dislike of apples began after she ate an apple, then felt unwell. Simone would like to be able to eat apples again without feeling a strong dislike.

1 Explain why Simone developed a dislike of apples. Use the terms in the box in your explanation.

conditioned   neutral   response   stimulus   unconditioned

2 Suggest how **imagery exposure therapy** could be used to help Simone like apples again.

KEY WORD

imagery exposure therapy: therapy in which the person is asked to vividly imagine their feared object, situation or activity

Exercise 9 Procedure

KEY WORD

quantitative data: numerical results about the amount or quantity of a psychological measure, such as pulse rate or a score on an intelligence test

This exercise will help you to demonstrate your knowledge of the procedure (including the research methods, experimental design, controls and research techniques for data collection) used by Saavedra and Silverman. Refer to Section 4.3 Core study 3 on Saavedra and Silverman's study in the coursebook or the original research paper to check your answers.

1   Think about the research method used in this study.

    a   Identify the research method.

    b   Describe how **one** other research method could be used to study treatment of phobias.

2   Think about when the study was conducted.

    a   When were the follow-up assessment sessions conducted?

    b   Explain why the assessment sessions were conducted.

3   Think about the variables that were measured.

    a   What quantitative data was collected in the study?

    b   Describe **one** example of quantitative data recorded in the study.

4   Think about the techniques used to measure these variables.

    a   How was the success of the treatment measured in the study?

    b   Explain the research method that was used in the study.

Exercise 10 Issues and debates

KEY WORDS

phobia: the irrational, persistent fear of an object or event (stimulus) that poses little real danger but creates anxiety and avoidance in the sufferer

objectivity: the impact of an unbiased external viewpoint on, for example, how data is interpreted. Interpretation is not affected by an individual's feelings, beliefs or experiences, so should be consistent between different researchers

subjectivity: the effect of an individual's personal viewpoint on, for example, how they interpret data. Interpretation can differ between individual researchers as a viewpoint may be biased by one's feelings, beliefs or experiences, so is not independent of the situation

KEY WORDS

mean: the measure of central tendency calculated by adding up the values of all the scores and dividing by the number of scores in the data set

This exercise will enable you to consider the issues and debates relevant to Saavedra and Silverman's study. It will also allow you to check your understanding of how to evaluate the study in terms of its strengths and weaknesses.

1   Name the issue or debate that is most relevant to each statement in the table about Saavedra and Silverman's study. Describe **one** way in which each statement relates to the issue or debate you have named.

Statement about the study	Relevant issue/debate	How the issue/debate relates to the statement about the study
a The little boy's **phobia** was considered to be acquired as a result of a negative experience.	i	ii
b The participant was a 9 year old boy.	i	ii
c To help treat people with phobias, feelings of fear and disgust must also be managed.	i	ii

2   The study was based on a single participant. Explain **one** disadvantage of using a **case study**.

3   Consider all your answers to Q1 and Q2. Analyse the study in terms of validity.

KEY WORD

case study: a research method in which a single instance, e.g. one person, family or institution, is studied in detail

RESEARCH METHODS

This exercise considers the types of data used in the three core studies in the learning approach. It will help you to describe the data collected in the studies.

1   Define what is meant by:

   a   quantitative data

   b   qualitative data

2   **a**   Outline **one** advantage and **one** disadvantage of each type of data shown in the table.

   b   Give **one** example of each type of data from one of the studies in the learning approach.

RESEARCH METHODS

Some information is given to get you started.

Type of data	Advantage	Disadvantage	Example from study
Quantitative	*Data is easier to analyse.*	**a i**	*Pass percentage for each trunk wash task in the study by Fagen et al.* **b i**
Qualitative	**a ii**	*Data is more time-consuming to analyse.*	*The interview data, for example on the boy's traumatic experience of spilled buttons in the study by Saavedra and Silverman.* **b ii**

3   Explain whether the data types are objective or subjective. Refer to at least one of the studies from the learning approach in your answer.

TIP

The concepts of **objectivity** and **subjectivity** are debated within psychology. Although objectivity is often seen as an important scientific aim, sometimes subjectivity can offer insight into the reasons or explanations for behaviour.

ISSUES AND DEBATES

This exercise will help you to consider how each of the core studies in the learning approach relates to a particular psychological issue and debate.

1   Use evidence from each core study to support both explanations of behaviour in the **nature–nurture** debate.

Core study	Nature explanation	Nurture explanation
a Bandura et al. (aggression)	i	ii
b Fagen et al. (elephant learning)	i	ii
c Saavedra and Silverman (button phobia)	i	ii

Chapter 5

Social approach

LEARNING INTENTIONS

In this chapter you will practise how to:

- describe and apply the concepts and terminology of the social approach and its main assumptions

- explain and apply the psychology being investigated in the social approach

- describe, evaluate and apply the three core studies from the social approach

- apply relevant research methods to the social approach

- consider issues and debates that are relevant to the social approach.

Exercise 1 Assumptions of the social approach

Each of the four approaches that you are studying has a set of underlying assumptions that guide the particular area of psychology and the research methods it uses. This exercise will enable you to demonstrate your understanding of the main assumptions of the social approach.

Tanya is at home preparing to give a presentation to her class. She has noticed that she feels nervous when she stands up, reads her presentation aloud and visualises her classmates as the audience.

1   Suggest the main assumption of the social approach that is relevant to Tanya's situation.

2   Explain why Tanya becomes nervous imagining giving her presentation, using the assumption you have suggested in question 1.

5.1 Core study 1: Milgram (obedience)

Exercise 2 Background

KEY WORDS

authority: a person or organisation in a position of power who can give orders and requires obedience

individual–situational debate: this is the debate about the relative influence or interaction of a person's unique physiology or personality (individual) and factors in the environment (situational) on thinking and behaviour

This exercise considers the background relevant to Milgram's study. It will also enable you to consider the context in which the study was conducted.

1   **a**   Define what is meant by the term 'obedience'.

    b   Describe **one** example in which being obedient can have a positive consequence.

2   Outline the historical event involving destructive obedience that led to Milgram's research.

3   Explain whether Milgram believed destructive obedience can be explained by individual or situational factors.

Exercise 3 Procedure

> **KEY WORD**
>
> **authority:** a person or organisation in a position of power who can give orders and requires obedience

This exercise will help you to show your knowledge of the procedure (including the sample size, demographics and sampling technique, controls, and the research techniques for data collection) used by Milgram. Refer to Section 5.1 Core study 1 on Milgram's study in the coursebook or the original research paper to check your answers.

1   Think about the research method used in the study.

    a   Identify the research method used in this study.

    b   Explain why this study would not be considered an experiment.

2   Think about where the study was conducted.

    a   Where did the study take place?

    b   Explain the choice of location.

3   Think about the variables that were measured.

    a   What **qualitative data** was collected in the study?

    b   Describe **one** of the behaviours recorded as qualitative data.

4   Think about the techniques used to measure these variables.

    a   How was the obedience of the participants recorded in the study?

    b   Explain the research method that was used in the study.

> **KEY WORD**
>
> **qualitative data:** descriptive, in-depth results indicating the *quality* of a psychological characteristic, such as responses to open questions in self-reports or case studies and detailed observations

> **TIP**
>
> Make sure you are clear in your responses about the different roles of the teacher (the participant), the learner (the confederate or victim) and the experimenter (the **authority** figure).

Exercise 4 Ethical issues

This exercise will allow you to consider the ethical guidelines and issues relevant to Milgram's study, and enable you to evaluate the study in terms of its ethical strengths and weaknesses.

1   Copy and complete the table. For each feature of the study, identify a relevant **ethical guideline** that could either have been broken or followed in the study and describe why each feature was or was not an **ethical issue**.

Feature of the study	Ethical issue	Ethical guideline
a Some participants showed signs of tension while delivering shocks.	i	ii
b The confederate was shown to be unharmed after the study.	i	ii
c The experimenter gave prods to participants, telling them they must continue.	i	ii
d Participants were told that the aim of the study was to see how punishment affects learning.	i	ii

2   For each ethical guideline you have identified as broken in question 1, suggest why this feature was necessary to achieve valid results.

5.2 Core study 2: Perry et al. (personal space)

Exercise 5 Aims

KEY WORDS

empathy: how people respond to the observed experiences of others, seeing or imagining experiences from the other person's point of view and feeling concerned or upset for them

interpersonal distance (personal space): the relative distance between people. It is the area of space around a person in which they prefer not to have others enter.

oxytocin: a social hormone found in humans that heightens the importance of social cues and is linked to positive social behaviours like helping others

---

In this exercise, you will consider the aim of the study, including the contextual difference between Experiment 1 and Experiment 2.

KEY WORD

differential effect: when one or more individuals experience a difference in outcome when exposed to the same stimuli

1 Complete the following sentence, filling in the gaps using the words from the box.

The aim of Perry et al. was to see whether **a** .... has a

differential effect on preferred **b** .... distance, depending on

how **c** .... a person is.

---

empathetic   interpersonal   **oxytocin**

---

2 State which of the following contexts were used in Experiment 1 and Experiment 2:

a Intimate

b Approach-avoidance

TIP

Remember that although the study by Perry et al. contains two experiments, both have the same aim and conclusion.

Exercise 6 Results

KEY WORDS

oxytocin: a social hormone found in humans that heightens the importance of social cues and is linked to positive social behaviours like helping others

social cues: these are facial expressions or body language that people use to send messages to one another, for example a smile to indicate happiness

KEY WORD

empathy: how people respond to the observed experiences of others, seeing or imagining experiences from the other person's point of view and feeling concerned or upset for them

In this exercise, you will consider the results of the study, including detail from both Experiment 1 and Experiment 2.

Michael has read an article about the hormone oxytocin (OT). He tells Samu that OT is also known as the 'love' hormone as it makes people want to be close to all the people around them. Samu has studied OT in psychology and he suggests it does not always have this effect.

1   Is Michael correct when he says OT makes people want to be close to all the people around them? Use the results of Experiment 1 to justify your reasoning.

2   Suggest whether Michael or Samu is right about the effect of OT on individuals with different **empathy** traits. Use the results of Experiment 2 to support your explanation.

Exercise 7 Conclusions

KEY WORDS

interpersonal distance: the relative distances between people

social salience: the importance or attention someone gives to cues from other people, e.g. body language, interpersonal distance and expressions

differential effect: when one or more individuals experience a difference in outcome when exposed to the same stimuli

In this exercise, you will consider the conclusions of the study, relating to the influence of oxytocin (OT) on interpersonal distance preference.

1   What effect did giving participants OT have on **social cues**?

2   Did giving OT have the same or opposite effects on people with different empathy levels?

KEY WORD

social cues: these are facial expressions or body language which people use to send messages to one another, for example a smile to indicate happiness

TIP

The conclusion(s) of any study should relate closely to the aim of the study. In some cases, the wording will be very similar and will not contain actual data from the study.

5.3 Core study 3: Piliavin et al. (subway Samaritans)

Exercise 8 The psychology being investigated

This exercise will help you to show your understanding of the psychology investigated by Piliavin et al.

Victor was walking through a busy city centre and noticed a man sitting on the street corner asking others for money. When he got home, he told his sister how no passers-by were stopping to speak to the man or give him money.

1 Explain why passers-by did not stop to help the man on the street corner. Refer to '**bystander apathy**' and '**diffusion of responsibility**' in your explanation.

2 Suggest other reasons why passers-by might not want to stop and help the man.

Exercise 9 Procedure

> ### KEY WORDS
>
> **experimental design:** the way in which participants are allocated to levels of the independent variable
>
> **operational definition:** the clear description of a variable such that it can be accurately manipulated, measured or quantified, and the study can be replicated. This includes the way that the independent variable and dependant variable in experiments and the co-variables in correlations are described

> ### KEY WORDS
>
> **bystander apathy:** when a bystander does not show concern for a person in need
>
> **diffusion of responsibility:** when there are other people available to help in an emergency, an individual may be less likely to take action because they feel a reduced sense of personal responsibility

In this exercise, you will consider the procedure of the study, including the research methods used, experimental design, and the measured and manipulated variables.

1 Compare the similarities and differences between a laboratory experiment and a field experiment, using Piliavin et al. to support your explanation.

2 Did the study by Piliavin et al. use an independent or repeated measures design? Justify your answer using detail from the study.

3 Copy and complete the table with details of the measured (**dependent**) **variables** and manipulated (**independent**) **variables**. Some information has been given to get you started.

Type	Name of variable	Operational definition
a Dependent variable (DV)	*Level of bystander helping*	Quantitative measures: *Time in seconds for first passenger to help* i i iii iv Qualitative measure: v
b Independent variable (IV)	*Type of victim* i ii iii	*Drunk or ill* iv v vi

TIP

Make sure you are clear in your responses about how each variable was operationalised as a definition. Be precise: the confederate in Piliavin et al.'s study was drunk or ill, not 'old'. When possible, include units such as seconds or centimetres.

Exercise 10 Evaluation

KEY WORDS

reliability: the extent to which a procedure, task or measure is consistent, for example, that it would produce the same results with the same people on each occasion

validity: the extent to which the researcher is testing what they claim to be testing

sample: the group of people selected to represent the population in a study

This exercise will help you to consider the strengths and weaknesses of different elements of the study.

1   Consider each evaluative issue in the table. Explain how each issue was a strength of the study, a weakness of the study or both.

Issue	Strength/Weakness?	Explanation
a Replicability	i	ii
b Reliability	i	ii
c Validity	i	ii
d Sample	i	ii
e Ethics	i	ii

RESEARCH METHODS

Below are key words relevant to research methods used in the studies from the social approach. The exercise will enable you to describe the methodology used in the studies.

1   Match the key words to their correct definition.

Key words	Definition
a controls	i descriptive, in-depth results indicating the *quality* of a psychological characteristic, such as responses to open questions in self-reports or case studies and detailed observations
b demographics	ii ways to keep potential confounding variables constant, e.g. between levels of the independent variable, to ensure measured differences in the dependent variable are likely to be due to the independent variable, raising validity
c qualitative data	iii numerical results about the amount or quantity of a psychological measure, such as pulse rate or a score on an intelligence test
d quantitative data	iv the method used to obtain participants for a study from the population
e sample	v the characteristics of a population such as age, sex and ethnicity
f sampling technique	vi The group of people selected to represent a population in a study

2   Give **one** example from one of the studies in the social approach for each of the key words in question 1.

ISSUES AND DEBATES

This exercise will help you to consider how each of the core studies in the social approach relates to a particular psychological issue and debate.

1 Use evidence from each core study to support an explanation of each type of behaviour in the **individual–situational debate**.

Core study	Individual explanation	Situational explanation
a Milgram (obedience)	i	ii
b Perry et al. (personal space)	i	ii
c Piliavin et al. (subway Samaritans)	i	ii

KEY WORD

individual– situational debate: the debate about the relative influence or interaction of a person's unique physiology or personality (individual) and factors in the environment (situational) on thinking and behaviour

> Chapter 6

Clinical psychology

In this chapter you will practise how to:

- describe, evaluate and compare diagnostic criteria for schizophrenia and to describe and evaluate explanations and treatments of schizophrenia, including applying the findings of the topic area to the real world.

- describe, evaluate and compare diagnostic criteria for mood disorders and to describe and evaluate explanations and treatments of mood disorders, including applying the findings of the topic area to the real world.

- describe, evaluate and compare diagnostic criteria for impulse control disorders and to describe and evaluate explanations and treatments of impulse control disorders, including applying the findings of the topic area to the real world.

- describe, evaluate and compare diagnostic criteria for anxiety disorders and fear-related disorders and to describe and evaluate explanations and treatments of anxiety disorders and fear-related disorders, including applying the findings of the topic area to the real world.

- describe, evaluate and compare diagnostic criteria for obsessive–compulsive disorder and to describe and evaluate explanations and treatments of obsessive–compulsive disorder, including applying the findings of the topic area to the real world.

6.1 Schizophrenia

Exercise 1 Diagnostic criteria for schizophrenia

KEY WORD

ICD-11: the 11th edition of the International Classification of Diseases. This is the global standard for coding health information and includes both physical and mental health disorders. It was developed and is updated by the World Health Organisation (WHO)

You need to know the diagnostic guidelines (ICD-11) for schizophrenia. This exercise will enable you to demonstrate your understanding of the symptoms of schizophrenia. It will also allow you to apply your knowledge to a scenario.

Tristan is a 20-year-old university student. He has been missing lectures and suddenly broken up with his girlfriend. Tristan shares a house with three other students and when his housemates ask him what is wrong, he barely responds or expresses how he feels. Tristan's housemates have become increasingly concerned about him as he is sometimes difficult to understand – he can be incoherent and change from one subject to another without warning. Tristan's housemates have contacted his parents as he has started to talk about how the government is broadcasting his thoughts to everyone and that he cannot protect his family from this. Tristan refers to the 'voices in his head' as giving a running commentary on his behaviour.

1   Outline **two** positive symptoms of schizophrenia that are evident in Tristan.

2   Outline **two** negative symptoms of schizophrenia that are evident in Tristan.

TIP

When answering application questions, make sure you refer directly to the question's scenario in your answer. You can use quotes from the scenario to show that you are able to apply your understanding.

Exercise 2 Explanations of schizophrenia

KEY WORDS

family study: a type of study investigating whether biological relatives of those with a disorder are more likely than non-biological relatives to be similarly affected

twin study: a type of study that compares sets of twins to analyse similarities and differences. This may include concordance for intelligence or mental disorders. Both monozygotic (MZ) and dizygotic (DZ) twins are studied, and their concordance rate is compared

adoption study: a type of study looking at the similarities between adopted individuals and their biological parents as a way of investigating the differing influences of biology and environment

---

This exercise will allow you to consider the explanations of schizophrenia and how they relate to the nature versus nurture debate.

Alice and Carlos are discussing the causes of schizophrenia. Carlos refers to someone he knows and says: 'He has got schizophrenia and so has his mum, so it must be genetic.' Alice believes it is not as simple as Carlos thinks.

1   Explain why Alice might be correct.

2   Suggest how the nature versus nurture debate could be applied to the explanations of schizophrenia.

3   Describe how **adoption studies** could be used to help our understanding of the biological versus environmental causes of schizophrenia.

TIP

When considering explanations of a disorder, it is important to remember that no explanation is likely to be a complete explanation. It may be useful to consider the interactionist approach as a more valid explanation – that biological and psychological causes may interact with each other.

Exercise 3 Treatment and management of schizophrenia

This exercise will allow you to consider the differences between typical and atypical antipsychotics.

1 Complete the table.

		Typical antipsychotics	Atypical antipsychotics
a	When they were developed	i	ii
b	Symptoms they can treat	i	ii
c	How they work	i	ii
d	Side-effects	i	ii

6.2 Mood (affective) disorders: depressive disorder (unipolar) and bipolar disorder

Exercise 4 Diagnostic criteria for mood (affective) disorders

KEY WORD

Beck Depression Inventory (BDI): this is the world's most widely used measure of depression, where respondents are asked how much they agree with a range of statements

This exercise will help you check your knowledge of the different types of episodes that may be evident in an individual with bipolar disorder.

1   Match each type of episode to its correct definition.

Type of episode	Definition
a manic episode	**i** a period of two weeks where there is a mixture of manic and depressive states
b mixed episode	**ii** a less extreme version of a manic episode and involves several days of persistent elevated mood or increased irritability
c depressive episode	**iii** a period of at least one week where mood is extremely high
d hypomanic episode	**iv** a period of at least two weeks and involves depressed mood or lack of interest in usual activities for most of the day, nearly every day

2   If someone is diagnosed with Type 1 Bipolar disorder, which of the episodes in question 1 might they experience?

3   **The Beck Depression Inventory (BDI)** asks the person taking the test to choose which statement they most agree with, out of four or more options. A higher score is associated with depression. What score, between 0 and 3, would be given to the following four statements?

   a   I don't get real satisfaction out of anything anymore.

   b   I get as much satisfaction out of things as I used to.

   c   I am dissatisfied and bored with everything.

   d   I don't enjoy things the way I used to.

Exercise 5 Explanations of mood (affective) disorders: depressive disorder (unipolar)

This exercise will allow you to check your knowledge of the key study by Oruč et al. (1997).

1   Outline the aim of the study by Oruč et al.

2   Outline the sample used by Oruč et al.

3   Evaluate the study by Oruč et al.

Exercise 6 Treatment and management of mood (affective) disorders

KEY WORDS

inhibit: to hinder or prevent. In neuropsychology, inhibition occurs when a chemical or chemical process is reduced or stopped

stoicism: a philosophy where one of the principles is that the individual is not directly affected by outside things but by their own *perception* of external things

This exercise will allow you to demonstrate your ability to evaluate treatments of mood disorders.

1   Complete the table, giving **one** strength and **one** weakness of biological treatments and psychological therapies for mood disorders.

		Biological treatments, including tricyclics, MAOIs, SSRIs	Psychological therapies, including Beck's cognitive restructuring, Ellis's rational emotive behaviour therapy (REBT)
a	Strength	i	ii
b	Weakness	i	ii

> **TIP**
>
> When evaluating treatments for any disorder, you need to consider the strengths and weaknesses in terms of both the effectiveness (how well the treatment or therapy works) and the appropriateness (the impact on the individual, such as any side-effects).

2   Patients are often treated with antidepressants as well as a psychological therapy. Explain why this might be the best approach.

3   State what the A, B and C stand for in Ellis's REBT.

A	
B	
C	

6.3 Impulse control disorders

Exercise 7 Diagnostic criteria for impulse control disorders

KEY WORDS

duration: the length of time something lasts, for example how long symptoms have been present

severity: the extent of something, or how bad it is. For example, symptoms may be mild, moderate or severe

This exercise will allow you to demonstrate your understanding of the diagnostic criteria for kleptomania, pyromania and gambling disorder.

1 For each of the cases, state whether the individual *could* be diagnosed with either kleptomania, pyromania, gambling disorder or none of them.

Case	Diagnosis
a Maggie has lost her job and is struggling to pay her bills, so she has started stealing food from the local shop.	
b Jonas started gambling just over a year ago. He now stays up late into the night gambling online, even though it causes arguments with his partner and makes him late for work the next day.	
c Daniel started burning things when he was young. As an adult, he has set fire to abandoned houses and shops. He watches as firefighters put out the fires.	
d Sofia stole dog food from the supermarket. She does not own a dog. She felt a buzz of excitement afterwards. She has since stolen several more items and now finds it impossible to resist the urge to steal.	
e April went to a casino with friends for her birthday. She was very excited when she was on a winning streak. She also lost some money, but overall had a lovely evening and is looking forward to visiting the casino again in a couple of months.	
f Jing got fired from his job. He blamed his manager who Jing always thought did not like him and was just waiting for a chance to fire him. Jing got so angry that he went to the manager's house and set fire to his car.	

2 For each of the individuals that you think would *not* be diagnosed with anything, give a reason why.

3 Which **one** of the following is the correct name for the measure of kleptomania?

A K-PAP

B K-SAS

C S-KAK

> **TIP**
>
> When answering questions about diagnostic criteria for a disorder, remember to include more than just the symptoms, such as **duration** and **severity** of symptoms, the effect on other aspects of life and what the symptoms are *not* attributed to, for example substance abuse.

Exercise 8 Explanations of impulse control disorders

KEY WORD

positive reinforcement: when a behaviour results in a reward, such as money or attention, that behaviour is likely to be repeated again

The multiple choice questions that follow will help you to check your knowledge of the explanations of impulse control disorders.

For each question, select **one** option.

1 a Which neurotransmitter is most associated with the onset of impulse control disorders?

   A serotonin   **B** dopamine   **C** glutamate

   b Activity in which part of the brain is most associated with impulse control disorders?

   A logical thinking   **B** disorganised speech   **C** reward and behavioural control

   c Kleptomania can be a side-effect of the treatment used for:

   A Parkinson's   **B** Alzheimer's   **C** epilepsy

2 a **Positive reinforcement** is one explanation for impulse control disorders. It is one aspect of:

   A classical conditioning   **B** operant conditioning   **C** psychoanalysis

   b Positive reinforcement comes from which approach?

   A cognitive   **B** biological   **C** behavioural

   c What term refers to the idea that gambling only leads to positive reinforcements some of the time?

   A intermittent reinforcement   **B** schedules of positivity   **C** schedules of reinforcement

3 a Who proposed the feeling–state theory?

   A Miller   **B** Freud   **C** Beck

   b The sensations, emotions and thoughts a person experiences in relation to a particular event is called:

   A drive   **B** feeling–state   **C** fixation

   c If setting a fire leads to the positive belief of 'I'm so powerful', which of the following is the *most likely* underlying negative belief?

   A I'm weak.   **B** I'm a winner.   **C** I'm unattractive.

Exercise 9 Psychological treatments of impulse control disorders

This exercise will enable you to check your knowledge and understanding of covert sensitisation as a treatment for impulse control disorders, and to apply the treatment to a specific impulse control disorder.

1   Complete the table, showing how covert sensitisation could be used to treat someone with pyromania.

Aspect of covert sensitisation	Description
a Imagery to be used	
b Relaxation technique	
c Visualisations	
d Homework	
e Association that is made	

6.4 Anxiety disorders and fear-related disorders

Exercise 10 Diagnostic criteria for anxiety disorders and fear-related disorders

This exercise will allow you to check your understanding of the diagnostic criteria for generalised anxiety disorder, agoraphobia and specific phobia (blood-injection-injury).

1   Complete each of the paragraphs. Fill in the gaps using words or phrases from each box.

a

> several months   substance or medication
> family, social or occupational   anxiety   health, family finances or work

Generalised anxiety disorder is characterised by marked symptoms of
i .... for most days, over a period of at least
ii .... The anxiety may be a general feeling of
apprehension or may be worry focused on multiple everyday events such as
iii .... Related symptoms such as muscular
tension, sleep disturbance, difficulty concentrating or irritability may also be
present. Symptoms result in significant distress or significant impairment in
one or more important areas of functioning such as
iv .... For a diagnosis to be made, the symptoms
must not be due to another medical condition or the effect of **v** ....
....

b

> panic attacks   fear   home   public transport
> actively avoided   anxiety

Agoraphobia is characterised by excessive **i** .... or
ii .... in response to situations where escape
might be difficult or help might not be available, such as using
iii .... , being in crowds or being outside the
iv .... alone. The person will be afraid of having specific
negative outcomes, such as **v** .... or other embarrassing
symptoms in a public place. When possible, these situations are
vi .... and only entered under specific circumstances or
endured with extreme distress. The symptoms persist for several months and
are severe enough to result in significant distress or significant impairment to
one or more important areas of functioning.

c

> disproportionate   fear or anxiety   severe
> blood, injection or injury

Specific phobia (blood-injection-injury) is characterised by excessive fear
or anxiety that occurs consistently when exposed to, or in anticipation of,
a specific stimulus, in this case the exposure to or anticipation of the
sight of **i** .... The fear or anxiety will be
ii .... to the actual danger and the phobic stimulus will
be avoided where possible or endured with intense
iii .... The symptoms persist for several months and
are **iv** .... enough to result in significant distress or
significant impairment to one or more important areas of functioning.

Exercise 11 Explanations of anxiety disorders and fear-related disorders

In this exercise, you will apply your knowledge of explanations of anxiety and fear-related disorders.

Suchitra has a phobia of birds. When she was young, a bird flew into her face, causing her to fall off her bicycle and break her arm.

1   Use the table to apply your knowledge of explanations of phobias to explain how Suchitra's phobia may have developed.

Before conditioning	unconditioned stimulus (UCS) a	→	unconditioned response (UCR) b
During conditioning	neutral stimulus (NS) + unconditioned stimulus (UCS) c	→	unconditioned response (UCR) d
After conditioning	conditioned stimulus (CS) e	→	conditioned response (CR) f

2   What is meant by a phobia becoming 'generalised'? Refer to the example of Suchitra's bird phobia to explain your answer.

3   Explain how Suchitra's phobia has continued into adulthood. Use the terms 'negative reinforcement' and 'avoidance' in your answer.

TIP

When referring to a term with a commonly used **abbreviation** (such as UCS for unconditioned stimulus), you should write the word or phrase in full the first time, followed by the abbreviation in brackets. Then you can use the abbreviation for the rest of the answer.

Exercise 12 Treatment and management of anxiety disorders and fear-related disorders

KEY WORDS

in vitro: instances where exposure to the phobic stimulus is imagined, such as through a visualisation exercise

in vivo: instances when the individual is directly exposed to the stimulus in real life

This exercise will allow you to demonstrate your knowledge and understanding of the treatments of anxiety and fear-related disorders. You will also apply your knowledge to specific examples.

1   Match each component of systematic desensitisation to its correct definition.

Component of systemic desensitisation		Definition	
a	reciprocal inhibition	i	a list of anxiety-provoking situations relating to the phobia that increase in severity
b	anxiety hierarchy	ii	replacing a conditioned response, such as fear, with another response, such as a feeling of calm
c	counter conditioning	iii	the impossibility of holding two strong and opposing emotions simultaneously
d	relaxation techniques	iv	these include muscle relaxation exercises, visualisation or even anti-anxiety drugs

2   Create an anxiety hierarchy of 6–10 stages for a patient who is trying to overcome a phobia of dogs.

3   a   Explain why systematic desensitisation could be an effective treatment for blood-injection-injury phobia.

    b   Explain why applied tension is specifically used to treat blood-injection-injury phobia.

6.5 Obsessive–compulsive disorder

Exercise 13 Diagnostic criteria for obsessive–compulsive disorder

This exercise will help you to check your knowledge and understanding of the diagnostic criteria for obsessive–compulsive disorder (OCD). In question 3, you will apply your knowledge to a scenario.

1 Decide whether each of the following statements is true or false.

    a Obsessions are repetitive behaviours.

    b For a diagnosis to be made, the obsessions and compulsions must take up more than an hour per day.

    c Repeatedly checking the lights are switched off is an example of a compulsion.

    d Beck Depression Inventory (BDI) is a measure used to assess obsessive–compulsive disorder.

    e Y-BOCS stands for Yale–Brown Obsessive Compulsive Scale.

2 How do you think someone with obsessive–compulsive disorder might answer each of the following true/false statements (from the Maudsley Obsessive–Compulsive Inventory – MOCI)?

    a I frequently have to check things (gas or water taps, doors, etc.) several times.

    b I am not unduly concerned about germs and diseases.

    c I do not take a long time to dress in the morning.

    d Even when I do something very carefully, I often feel that it is not quite right.

3 Luisa was diagnosed with obsessive–compulsive disorder one year ago. Before she was diagnosed, she did not want to admit to herself or to her partner or family that she had a problem. She has become distanced from her friends and stopped her hobbies because it became too difficult for her to hide her compulsions.

Luisa washes her hands dozens of times a day and worries that her children will become seriously ill if she does not wash her hands for the correct number of times in the correct sequence.

Luisa has intrusive thoughts about her children becoming unwell or getting hurt, so she finds it difficult to take them outside to play or to visit friends or family.

Luisa finds it difficult to manage her job as an accountant because she finds it more difficult to manage her compulsions when in the office. Her partner thinks she should leave her job and try to find work she can do from home.

Explain how Luisa's obsessive–compulsive disorder might have a significant impact on the following important areas of functioning:

    a Family

    b Social

    c Occupational

> **TIP**
>
> When reading a question, particularly one with a scenario, highlight or underline key words. This will enable you to pick out the information that you may need for your answer.

Exercise 14 Explanations of obsessive-compulsive disorder

This exercise will allow you to check your knowledge of the different explanations of OCD.

1   Match the neurotransmitter to its correct description.

Neurotransmitter	Description
a Dopamine	i There is mixed evidence of the role of this neurotransmitter in people with OCD.
b Serotonin	ii People with OCD tend to have abnormally high levels of this neurotransmitter.
c Oxytocin	iii People with OCD tend to have lower than normal levels of this neurotransmitter.

2   Identify which statements relate to the genetic, cognitive–behavioural or psychodynamic explanation of OCD.

Statement	Explanation
a Obsessive thinking is based on faulty reasoning.	
b MZ twins have a higher concordance rate for OCD than DZ twins.	
c OCD may result from tension between children and their parents.	
d OCD can result from becoming fixated in one of the psychosexual stages.	
e Compulsions can be explained through operant conditioning: the compulsion is seen as 'reward' as it temporarily relieves the worry.	
f It is known that serotonin and dopamine levels are implicated in OCD. This explanation looks to understand what causes these changes in neurotransmitters.	

Exercise 15 Treatment and management of Obsessive-compulsive disorder

> **KEY WORDS**
>
> **meta-analysis:** data from a range of studies into the same subject is combined and analysed to get an overall understanding of the trends
>
> **habituated:** when a person becomes accustomed to something. When someone is frequently exposed to a certain stimulus then over time, they become used to it.

This exercise will help you to check your knowledge and understanding of the treatments of obsessive–compulsive disorder (OCD).

1   Complete the table. Name the explanation for obsessive–compulsive disorder that best matches each of the treatments. Give a brief justification for your answer. You can use the same explanation more than once.

Treatment	Explanation	Justification for answer
a Selective serotonin reuptake inhibitors (SSRIs)	i	ii
b Exposure response prevention (ERP)	i	ii
c Cognitive–behavioural therapy (CBT)	i	ii

2   Complete the following paragraphs about SSRIs as a treatment of obsessive–compulsive disorder. Fill in the gaps using the words from the box.

> antidepressants   anxiety   dosage   higher   neuron
> reabsorbed   serotonin   severity   SSRIs

OCD can be treated with a range of different drug therapies, including

a .... and anti-anxiety medication. The most used

medications to treat OCD are **b** .... These medications work

by blocking the **c** .... from being **d** ....

once a message has been passed from one **e** .... to another,

meaning levels remain **f** ....

The effect of taking SSRIs to treat OCD is that they reduce the

g .... of obsessive–compulsive symptoms as they seem to

lessen the **h** .... associated with the disorder. They have been shown to work in individuals with and without depression, although generally a higher **i** .... of medication is given as it has been shown to be more effective.

3 Complete the following sentences to describe ERP as a treatment for obsessive–compulsive disorder.

    a ERP stands for _____

    b ERP is a form of _____

    c Individuals are exposed to the stimuli that _____

    d At the same time, individuals are helped to _____

    e The individual learns to _____

    f It is essential to prevent the compulsive behaviour as a response to the obsessive thought so the individual can learn that _____

RESEARCH METHODS

This exercise will enable you to apply your understanding of research methods. It will also help you to design a study.

1 Define the following terms:

    a Randomised control trial

    b Independent measures

    c Control group

    d Validity

    e Reliability

2 Using the key study by Lovell et al. (2006) to help you, design a study to compare the effectiveness of CBT and SSRIs as a treatment for OCD.

You should consider:

- the aim(s) and hypotheses of the study
- the independent and dependent variable(s)
- the design of the study, including:
  - research method(s) used
  - sample
  - sampling technique
  - experimental design
  - controls
  - research technique for data collection.

3 **a** Analyse the study you have designed. Discuss **one** strength and **one** weakness of the study.

    b Consider **one** way in which you might improve your study.

TIP

When considering how a study could be improved, think about where the weaknesses lie and consider alternatives. For example, there is likely to be a compromise between how realistic a study is and how well controlled it is, so consider which is more important.

ISSUES AND DEBATES

This exercise will help you to check your understanding of the nomothetic versus idiographic debate in psychology, and to apply your knowledge.

1   Decide whether each of the following statements applies to a nomothetic or an idiographic approach.

   a   This approach is concerned with what we share with others.

   b   This approach is scientific as it uses objective measures and controlled methods, meaning results can be replicated and generalised.

   c   This approach is very time-consuming as it involves in-depth research into an individual.

   d   This approach can be seen as losing sight of the 'whole person'.

   e   This approach is interested in what makes us unique.

   f   This approach tends to involve quantitative data.

   g   This approach tends to involve qualitative data.

   h   This approach considers the impact of free will.

2   Give **one** example of when a nomothetic approach was taken and **one** example of when an idiographic approach was taken in Clinical psychology. (You may wish to refer to Chapter 6 of the coursebook.)

3   Why might it be beneficial to consider both the nomothetic and idiographic approaches together, rather than focusing on one or the other?

TIP

When you are considering a psychological debate, remember to think about the strengths and weaknesses of each side of the debate and then think about whether it is more appropriate to consider both sides together rather than one or the other.

> Chapter 7

Consumer psychology

LEARNING INTENTIONS

In this chapter you will practise how to:

- describe, evaluate and compare research into the influence of the physical environment in consumer psychology, including applying the findings of the topic area to the real world.

- describe, evaluate and compare research into the influence of the psychological environment in consumer psychology, including applying the findings of the topic area to the real world.

- describe, evaluate and compare theories behind consumer decision-making, and to evaluate them, including applying the findings of the topic area to the real world.

- describe, evaluate and compare psychological theories on selling, buying and gifting of products, including applying the findings of the topic area to the real world.

- describe, evaluate and compare research into advertising, including applying the findings of the topic area to the real world.

7.1 The physical environment

Exercise 1 Retail store design

This exercise will allow you to demonstrate your knowledge and understanding of the three main layouts of store interior design.

1   Draw the three main layouts of store interior design.

a Grid layout	b Freeform layout	c Racetrack layout

2   Suggest a type of shop that would best suit:

  a   a grid layout

  b   a freeform layout

  c   a racetrack layout

3   For each type of store interior design, evaluate by giving **one** strength and **one** weakness.

Store interior design	Strength	Weakness
a Grid layout	i	ii
b Freeform layout	i	ii
c Racetrack layout	i	ii

TIP

When evaluating strengths and weaknesses, it is helpful to remember that the strength of one design/model/theory often highlights a weakness of another.

Exercise 2 Sound and consumer behaviour

The multiple choice questions below will help you to check your knowledge of the effect of sound on consumer behaviour.

For each question, select **one** option.

1   What type of experiment was North et al.'s (2003) study?

A   lab experiment

B   observation

C   field experiment

2   Which of the following was *not* a key finding of the study by North et al. (2003)?

A   total spend was higher when classical music was played, compared to pop music.

B   customers spent more on coffee when pop music was played, compared to classical music.

C   there was a significant difference between conditions for spending on starters, coffees, total food and total overall spend.

3   Which of the following is *not* a possible explanation for the influence of sound on taste?

A   imprinting

B   implicit association

C   attentional

Exercise 3 Retail atmospherics

This exercise will allow you to apply your knowledge of the pleasure-arousal-dominance (PAD) model, as well as the effect of perceived crowding, to a scenario.

Three friends are discussing separate shopping trips to the same shopping centre during the school holidays.

Harpreet says: 'I stayed all day; it was really good. It was so busy with lots of people – I found it really exciting and stimulating to be around so many people having a good time. I thought the shops were laid out well and I could get past people easily enough.'

Maja says: 'I didn't enjoy it. The centre was too busy. There were so many people and it made me feel quite anxious. Also, I didn't manage to get to all the shops I had planned to visit because everything took too long, so that was disappointing.'

Liam says: 'I went at the end of the day. The centre was quiet and there were few shoppers. Most of the time was good, but in one shop the staff were rearranging and there were boxes and rails cluttering up the shop floor. I didn't stay there long.'

1 Explain the difference between Maja's and Liam's experiences. Refer to the different types of perceived crowding in your answer.

2 Explain the key differences between Harpreet and Maja that affected their experience. Refer to the PAD model in your answer.

3 Their friend Cara says she planned to go to the shopping centre at the weekend but wondered if it might be too busy. What advice could the three friends give Cara?

7.2 The psychological environment

Exercise 4 Environmental influences on consumers

This exercise will allow you to demonstrate your knowledge of the four types of trip and the five types of spatial behaviour patterns used by consumers in stores.

1 For each description, name the correct type of trip.

Trip	Description
a	Moving up and along the top corridor, then returning along the main corridor with detours into various aisles.
b	Linear progression along the main corridor, zigzagging through the aisles and mostly exiting near the far end of the store.

Trip	Description
c	A short, simple trip for a few targeted items, not necessarily visiting the most popular products.
d	Using the main corridor for entering and exiting the building, moving down various aisles, mostly the top aisles initially, then the bottom aisles on the return.

2   Match each spatial behaviour pattern to its correct description.

Spatial behaviour pattern	Description
a Specialist	i Involves fast movements and fast decisions, shows preference for the main corridor but going where necessary. This spatial behaviour pattern has the highest proportion of male shoppers, and includes mainly people who are on a 'top-up' or 'food for tonight' mission.
b Native	ii A long trip visiting relevant aisles. Interactions are most likely to lead to purchases. Shoppers are mainly on a 'main' or 'top-up' mission.
c Tourist	iii The longest trip, visiting all aisles in the store and often visiting places more than once. This involves spending a long time with products and buying a lot. Involves a 'main' shopping mission.
d Explorer	iv Focuses on a few products, spending a lot of time with each product, though not necessarily resulting in a purchase. Shoppers are mainly on a 'top-up' or 'non-food' mission.
e Raider	v Fastmoving shoppers who do not stray too far from the entrance and tend to stay in the main corridor. They look more than buy; some are on a 'non-food' mission.

3   a   Which type of spatial pattern behaviour has the highest proportion of males?

    b   Which type of behaviour is most likely to have a shopping list?

    c   Which type of behaviour is most likely to use a trolley?

Exercise 5 Menu design psychology

This exercise will allow you to apply your knowledge of menu design, menu item position and effect of food name on food choice.

Three friends go out for lunch and each explains their decision of what they chose.

Aaron: 'It was in its own box on the menu, so it seemed like a good option.'

Razi: 'It was the first one that I read in the burger section, so it stuck in my mind.'

Gabriela: 'It was home-made and slow-cooked, which sounded tasty.'

1   Explain each of the three friends' choices, using your knowledge of consumer psychology.

2   Briefly describe the procedure and findings of one relevant study into menu item position.

3   Evaluate the use of a lab experiment to investigate aspects of consumer psychology like this.

TIP

When asked to briefly describe procedure and findings, try to think about someone who has not studied consumer psychology reading your description. Would your description give them a general understanding of what happened and what was found?

Exercise 6 Consumer behavior and personal space

KEY WORD

personal space: the physical space around someone, which they consider to be psychologically theirs

This exercise will enable you to check your knowledge of Hall's four zones and demonstrate your ability to apply your knowledge to specific situations.

1   Match each scenario to the appropriate zone and distance.

Scenario	Zone	Distance
a A guest lecturer giving a presentation	i Intimate	A 12 feet (3.7 m) or more
b A couple out for dinner at a restaurant	ii Personal	B 18 inches–4 feet (46–122 cm)
c Two good friends having a coffee	iii Social	C Less than 18 inches (46 cm)
d A meeting with colleagues	iv Public	D 4–12 feet (1.2–3.7 m)

2   Describe briefly **two** responses that someone may feel if another person invades their **personal space**.

7.3 Consumer decision-making

Exercise 7 Consumer decision-making

This exercise will allow you to check your knowledge and understanding of the models and strategies of decision-making.

1   Decide whether each of the following statements is true or false.

   a   Utility theory states that a decision is made rationally, based on optimising likely outcomes of their actions.

   b   Prospect theory proposes that a decision is made based on finding an option that is 'good enough'.

   c   The terms 'value' and 'endowment' are concepts within prospect theory.

2   Match each type of decision-making strategy to its correct definition.

Type of decision-making strategy		Definition	
a	compensatory	i	a strategy where each attribute is evaluated individually
b	non-compensatory	ii	a strategy where the value of one attribute can be allowed to compensate for another
c	partially compensatory	iii	a strategy where items are considered in relation to one another in terms of important attributes

Exercise 8 Choice heuristics

> **KEY WORD**
>
> **heuristics:** mental shortcuts that can help us when making decisions but can lead to errors in judgement

This exercise will enable you to apply your knowledge of different heuristics that can be used in decision-making.

1   For each description, name the correct heuristic.

Heuristic	Description
a	Comparing a new model of mobile phone to the current market leader.
b	Deciding not to buy a particular brand of mobile phone because your friend had one that broke.

Heuristic	Description
c	Deciding what phone to get based on its camera, as you consider this the most important feature.
d	Choosing a brand of mobile phone you know over an unknown brand even though the specifications are identical.
e	Deciding not to buy a certain brand of mobile phone because you read a poor review when you first started your research, even though everything you have read since is positive.

2　Why might it be useful for consumers to understand about different heuristics?

3　Why might it be useful for sellers to understand about different heuristics?

Exercise 9 Mistakes in decision-making

KEY WORD

Likert-type scale: a type of question used in surveys and questionnaires, where the respondent is asked to answer on a scale of, for example 1–7, the extent to which they agree with a range of statements

This exercise will allow you to test your knowledge of decision-making styles, and to consider how you would measure them.

1　Match each decision-making style to its correct definition.

Decision-making style		Definition	
a	rational	i	putting off decisions or making decisions only at the last minute
b	intuitive	ii	consulting others and relying on their assistance when making a decision
c	dependent	iii	making quick and impulsive decisions
d	avoiding	iv	making decisions that 'feel right'
e	spontaneous	v	making decisions in a logical way, where various options are considered to achieve a specific goal

2　Suggest **five** questions, using **Likert-type scales**, that you would include in a questionnaire to identify someone's decision-making style. One question should refer to each decision-making style.

3　Evaluate the use of using Likert-type scales by giving **one** strength and **one** weakness.

7.4 The product

Exercise 10 Packaging and positioning of a product

This exercise will help you to demonstrate your knowledge of the hypotheses and results of Becker et al. (2010), and to evaluate the study.

1   Identify the four hypotheses from Becker et al.'s study.

2   Describe the results of the study.

3   Give **one** strength and **one** limitation of the study.

> **TIP**
>
> Remember that hypotheses are different from aims. Hypotheses are specific statements with predictions that are going to be tested. Aims are more general descriptions of the intention of the study.

Exercise 11 Selling the product

The multiple choice questions below will help you to test your knowledge of sales techniques, interpersonal influence techniques and Cialdini's six ways to close a sale.

For each question, select **one** option.

1   Comparing yourself to other companies is:

    A   a customer-focused sales technique

    B   a competitor-focused sales technique

    C   a product-focused sales technique

2   DTR stands for:

    A   distress then rescue

    B   distort then release

    C   disrupt then reframe

3   NFCC stands for:

    A   need for choice closure

    B   need for cognitive closure

    C   not for cognitive conflict

Exercise 12 Buying the product

KEY WORD

cognitive dissonance: the feeling of discomfort that comes from holding two conflicting beliefs, or when there is a conflict between beliefs and behaviours

In this exercise, you will apply your knowledge of post-purchase cognitive dissonance to a scenario.

Yasmin and her daughter live a few miles from the nearest town. Yasmin's daughter studies hard and has a part-time job. Yasmin wanted to give her daughter a special present for her 18th birthday. She decided to buy her a car and looked for one that was eco-friendly since her daughter has strong beliefs about environmental issues. Yasmin overstretched her small budget and spent more than she had planned on a car that she liked but that was not environmentally friendly. Now, Yasmin is regretting her decision.

1   Analyse Yasmin's case by naming **three** factors that increase the likelihood of **cognitive dissonance** and explain why they may be relevant to Yasmin.

2   Explain **three** ways in which Yasmin's dissonance could be reduced. Refer to cognitive dissonance in your answer.

7.5 Advertising

Exercise 13 Types of advertising and advertising techniques

This exercise will allow you to check your knowledge and understanding of psychological research into types of adverts and advertising techniques

1   Decide whether each of the following statements about the Yale model of communication is true or false.

   a   The Yale model of communication was developed initially to understand wartime propaganda in the Second World War.

   b   The basic idea of the Yale model can be summarised as 'who said what, and when?'

   c   A message is more likely to be paid attention to if it is perceived as coming from someone with credibility.

   d   A message will be more effective if you focus just on the side of the argument you are taking.

   e   Individuals aged 18–25 are more likely to change their attitude.

2 Decide if each of the following statements about Lauterborn's 4Cs marketing mix model is true or false.

a The 4Cs model was developed to replace the 4Ts model.

b Cost to satisfy is one of the 4Cs.

c Credibility is one of the 4Cs.

d Convenience to buy corresponds to 'place' in the classic 4Ps model.

e Communication refers to a two-way conversation between the company and customer.

Exercise 14 Advertising–consumer interaction

This exercise will allow you to demonstrate your knowledge and understanding of Snyder and DeBono's (1985) study 3

1 Describe the aim of study 3 by Snyder and DeBono.

2 Describe the procedure of study 3 by Snyder and DeBono.

3 Summarise the results of study 3 by Snyder and DeBono.

Exercise 15 Brand awareness and recognition

KEY WORDS

slogan: a short memorable phrase used in advertising a product

logo: a symbol used by a company to act as a visual cue to allow faster processing and universal brand recognition across languages and cultures

brand name: the name used by a company to distinguish their products or services from other companies' products or services. It is their key identity and cannot be easily changed

This exercise will help you to check your knowledge of the importance of effective slogans and apply this knowledge to a scenario.

Karl and Mia are marketing a new brand of chocolate and they are discussing their views on **slogans**.

Mia says: 'A slogan is essential. The two most important things about the slogan are that it is simple, and that it is a jingle, because these two things will make it easier to remember.'

Karl replies: 'I don't think the slogan is that important. We have a good **logo** and a **brand name**. We can add a slogan later if we think we need one.

1 Who are you more likely to agree with? Why?

2 Analyse the opinions of Karl and Mia. Select **one** thing that Karl has said and **one** thing that Maya has said that is incorrect and explain why this is the case.

RESEARCH METHODS

This exercise will allow you to apply your understanding of research methods. It will also enable you to demonstrate your ability to design a study.

1   Define the following terms:

   a   Virtual reality

   b   Laboratory experiment

   c   Closed question

2   a   You have been asked to help design a shopping mall. Design a study to help with this project. Your study should be a laboratory experiment, use virtual reality and use closed questions.

   b   Evaluate your study by giving **two** strengths and **two** weaknesses of your study.

TIP

When evaluating a laboratory experiment, it can be helpful to compare it to a **field experiment**, as the strengths of one tend to be the weaknesses of another.

KEY WORD

field experiment: an investigation looking for a causal relationship in which an independent variable is manipulated and is expected to be responsible for changes in the dependent variable. It is conducted in the normal environment for the participants for the behaviour being investigated and some control of variables is possible

ISSUES AND DEBATES

This exercise will help you to check your understanding of cultural differences in psychology, and to apply your knowledge.

1   Decide whether the statements about cultural differences are true or false.

   a   There is an issue with a study that assumes all cultures are the same.

   b   A study carried out in one culture can never be useful to another culture.

   c   A study with a large sample cannot suffer from issues related to cultural differences.

2   a   Name **one** finding of del Campo et al.'s (2016) study that demonstrates cultural differences.

   b   Briefly explain why Sinha et al. (2002) carried out their study into store choice in India.

3   a   The vast majority of research into consumer psychology is carried out in the United States. Explain **one** problem with this, in terms of cultural differences.

   b   Explain **one** way of overcoming the issues surrounding cultural difference in consumer psychology research.

Chapter 8

Health psychology

LEARNING INTENTIONS

In this chapter you will practise how to:

- describe, evaluate and compare research into the patient–practitioner relationship, including applying the findings of the topic area to the real world.

- describe, evaluate and compare research into adherence to medical advice, including applying the findings of the topic area to the real world.

- describe, evaluate and compare research into pain, including applying the findings of the topic area to the real world.

- describe, evaluate and compare research into stress, including applying the findings of the topic area to the real world.

- describe, evaluate and compare research into health promotion, including applying the findings of the topic area to the real world.

8.1 The patient–practitioner relationship

Exercise 1 Practitioner and patient interpersonal skills

This exercise will allow you to check your knowledge of terms associated with practitioner and patient interpersonal skills.

1   Define the following terms:

    a   Non-verbal communication

    b   General practice

    c   Verbal communication

    d   Utilisers

    e   Under-utilisers

Exercise 2 Patient and practitioner diagnosis and style

This exercise will allow you to check your understanding of false positive and false negative diagnoses, and their implications.

1 Complete the table.

	Also known as a Type... error?	Is the patient unwell?	Are they given a diagnosis?
a False positive diagnosis	i	ii	iii
b False negative diagnosis	i	ii	iii

2 **a** Outline **one** danger of a false positive diagnosis.

b Outline **one** danger of a false negative diagnosis.

> **TIP**
>
> For key words such as false negative/false positive, where it is easy to muddle up the two, find a rhyme or some other way to remember the difference. Perhaps think of words that start with the first letter of each key word to help you remember the definitions.

Exercise 3 Misusing health services

This activity will allow you to demonstrate your knowledge and understanding of aspects of delay in seeking treatment.

1 Match each term to its correct definition.

Term	Definition
a appraisal delay	**i** the time the patient takes to appraise a symptom as a sign of illness. This involves deciding whether or not there is something wrong, i.e. that they are 'ill'
b illness delay	**ii** the time between when the patient decides they are ill and when they decide to seek medical care
c utilisation delay	**iii** the time from the decision to seek care until the patient accesses services. This can include the consideration of whether the costs of care (time, effort, money) are worth it

2 Give **one** factor that is likely to predict delay at each of the following stages:

  a Appraisal delay

  b Illness delay

  c Utilisation delay

8.2 Adherence to medical advice

Exercise 4 Types of non-adherence and reasons why patients don't adhere

This exercise will allow you to show your understanding of the different types of non-adherence, the reasons for non-adherence, as well as the implications of non-adherence.

1 Match the types of non-adherence to the correct definitions.

Type of non-adherence	Definition
a primary non-adherence	**i** this involves ways in which medication is not taken as prescribed. This may include missing doses, taking medication at incorrect times or taking incorrect doses
b non-persistence	**ii** this occurs when a doctor writes a prescription, but the medication is never collected, that is, the patient does not hand in the prescription to get the medication they have been prescribed
c non-conforming	**iii** this occurs when the patient starts to take the medication but stops without being advised to do so by a medical professional

2 For each of the problems **a–g** caused by non-adherence, state whether it is an implication for the individual, for medical services in general, or for both.

  a Waste of medication

  b Time lost due to missed appointments

  c Progression of illness

  d Reduced functional abilities

  e Lower quality of life

  f Increased use of medical resources

  g Impact on medical research

Exercise 5 Measuring non-adherence

This exercise will help you to check your knowledge and understanding of measures of non-adherence and to practise evaluation skills.

1   Complete the following sentences using **one** of the options.

    a MAM stands for:

        A Measuring Adherence to Medicine

        B Medical Adherence Measure

        C Medicine Assessment Measure

    b An example of a medication event monitoring system device is:

        A TestTub

        B TrackCap

        C MeasureLid

    c Pill counting means:

        A asking the patient to count how many pills they have left each day

        B counting how many pills the patient should take each day

        C asking the patient to bring in medication so it can be counted

2   Give **one** strength and **one** weakness of using a medication event monitoring system (MEMS) device.

3   **a** Give **one** reason why a blood sample might be a better measure of non-adherence than a MEMS device.

    b Give **one** reason why a MEMS device might be a better measure of non-adherence than a blood sample.

Exercise 6 Improving adherence

This exercise will allow you to check your understanding of the study by Yokley and Glenwick (1984), including the findings and conclusions they drew, as well as to be able to evaluate the research.

Kyra and Renato are discussing immunisations.

Kyra says: 'People will either immmunise their children or they won't. There is little anyone else can do about it.'

Renato disagrees but has no evidence to support his argument.

1   Use Yokley and Glenwick's findings about **community interventions** to help Renato support his point of view.

2   Give **two** strengths of Yokley and Glenwick's study to help Renato strengthen his case.

TIP

When considering strengths and weaknesses of measures or tests for people, consider the effectiveness as well as the practicalities involved. For example, a very effective test might be very inconvenient or invasive.

KEY WORD

community interventions: any attempts to encourage a certain behaviour in a town or city, using methods such as leafleting, letters and lotteries

TIP

When evaluating a study, always ask yourself, 'Why does this matter?' For example, one strength of a field experiment is that it is carried out in a natural setting. Why does this matter? Because the results are more realistic and can be applied beyond the research setting.

8.3 Pain

Exercise 7 Types and theories of pain

This exercise will allow you to compare two types of pain, and to check your knowledge of the theories of pain.

1   For each of the statements below, state whether it is referring to acute pain or chronic pain.

    a   It can be severe but comes on quickly.

    b   It usually results from long-term behavioural factors or illness.

    c   It lasts a relatively short period of time.

    d   It tends to be resistant to treatment.

    e   It is most common in the elderly, and the most common type is **musculoskeletal**.

    f   It is usually in a specific location with an obvious source.

    g   It lasts for at least a month.

    h   It can have a significant impact on quality of life.

    i   It is usually easy to treat.

> ### KEY WORD
>
> **musculoskeletal:** referring to the muscles, bones, ligaments and tendons in the body

2   Complete the paragraphs about theories of pain. Fill in the gaps using words from the boxes.

    a   Specificity theory proposes that there is a separate **i** .... system for processing pain, in the same way as there is for the senses such as **ii** .... and vision. Specialised pain **iii** .... respond to stimuli and, via nerve impulses, send signals to the brain. The brain then processes the signal as the sensation of **iv** .... , and quickly responds with a motor response to try to stop the pain. For example, if you touch something hot, the **v** .... from pain receptors in your hand travel up to your brain, to be processed as a pain sensation. The brain then sends a message back to the muscles in the hand, telling them to move the hand away from the source of the pain. This happens **vi** .... and almost instantaneously.

> receptors   sensory   nerve impulses
> automatically   hearing   pain

b   Gate control theory proposes that the spinal cord contains a

i .... that either prevents pain signals from entering the

brain or allows them to continue. This theory can explain why our emotional

state, or our ii .... , affect how much something hurts.

The gating mechanism occurs in the iii .... of the spinal

cord, where both small nerve fibres iv (.....................................) and large

nerve fibres (fibres for touch, pressure and other skin sensations) carry

information to. When there is more v .... fibre activity

compared to vi .... fibre activity people experience less

pain (the pain gates are closed). When there is more small fibre activity,

vii .... can be sent to the brain in order for pain to be

perceived (the pain gates are open). This explains why people rub injuries

after they happen, for example if you bang your elbow on a table you will rub

where it hurts for a few moments. The increase in normal

viii .... sensation (large fibres) inhibits the activity of the

pain fibres (small fibres) so pain perception is ix ....

> **TIP**
>
> It is important that you know key words from research. A good way of learning them is to write out terms and definitions on sticky notes and place them where you can see them regularly.

---

dorsal horn   touch   reduced   'gate'   pain fibres
large   small   expectations   pain signals

Exercise 8 Measuring pain

This exercise will allow you to check your understanding of different measures of pain, and to compare them to one another.

1   Complete the table, giving **one** strength and **one** weakness of each measure of pain.

Measure of pain	Strength	Weakness
a Clinical interview	i	ii
b McGill pain questionnaire	i	ii
c Visual analogue scale	i	ii
d UAB pain behaviour scale	i	ii

2   Decide whether each of the following statements about the study by Brudvik et al. (2017) is true or false.

   a   One of the aims was to measure the agreement of pain intensity when measured by children, parents and physicians.

   b   The Coloured Analogue scale was used for children aged 3–8 years old.

   c   Physicians' ratings of pain was highest.

   d   Parents' and children's pain ratings were closer than physicians' and children's pain ratings.

Exercise 9 Managing and controlling pain

This exercise will allow you to check your knowledge and understanding of biological and psychological treatments of pain.

1   For each of the following statements, identify which treatment of pain it is referring to.

Statement	Type of treatment
a This works by entering your blood stream and attaching to certain receptors in your brain.	
b This involves the insertion of very fine needles in the skin at specific points.	
c This involves the patient replacing threatening or negative thoughts about the pain with more rational or positive thoughts.	
d This reduces pain by reducing the production of the hormone-like substances that cause pain: **prostaglandins**.	
e This strategy involves the person thinking about a calm and relaxing situation or scene and focusing on this rather than the pain.	
f This sends electrical impulses to an area of pain and reduces the pain signals that go to the brain and spinal cord.	
g This strategy involves finding ways to shift attention away from the pain and onto something else instead.	

KEY WORD

prostaglandins: hormone-like substances that cause pain

8.4 Stress

Exercise 10 Sources of stress

This exercise will allow you to apply your knowledge of personality types as a source of stress.

Ahmed and Suki are talking about an article in a magazine about personality types and stress.

Ahmed says: 'I'm type B personality, so I don't need to worry about stress!'

Suki says: 'That's not right – there are plenty of things aside from personality that cause stress.'

1   To what extent do you agree with Ahmed? Use research to support your answer.

2   To what extent do you agree with Suki? Use research to support your answer.

> **TIP**
>
> When answering an application question, be selective about what information you use in your answer. Not all information surrounding the topic will be relevant, so think about the most important and relevant aspects.

Exercise 11 Measures of stress

This activity will allow you to check your knowledge and understanding of Holmes and Rahe's (1967) social readjustment rating scale.

The **social readjustment rating scale (SSRS)** provides quantitative data on life events.

1   Give **one** reason why quantitative data is a strength in this context.

2   Give **one** reason why quantitative data is a weakness in this context.

3   Using the example of marriage, explain why the assigned life change units (LCUs) might not be accurate for different people undergoing the same **life event**.

> **KEY WORDS**
>
> **social readjustment rating scale (SSRS):** a scale consisting of 43 life events; the respondent must identify any of the events they have experienced during a period of time. Each life event is given a score in terms of life change units (LCUs) and a total score is used to predict likelihood of stress-related illness
>
> **life events:** any major changes in your life (either positive or negative). The key aspect of a life event is that it requires some aspect of transition in your life

Exercise 12 Managing stress

This exercise will allow you to check your knowledge of stress inoculation training (SIT).

1 Complete the description of these three phases of **stress inoculation training (SIT)**. Fill in the gaps using words and phrases from the boxes.

a Conceptualisation: in this stage, the client and therapist work together to get an understanding of the client's **i** .... The client talks through their experiences and current method of dealing with stress. The therapist then shows the client how to **ii** .... a stressor as a problem that can be solved. It is important at this stage that the client understands that there are some parts of a **iii** .... that can be changed and some parts that cannot.

> reframe   sources of stress   stressor

b Skills acquisition and **i** .... : clients learn new **ii** .... skills, which are designed to suit their unique set of circumstances. Initially, the coping skills are practised in the therapy setting before being gradually applied in the **iii** ....
A range of cognitive and behavioural coping skills are taught, including problem-solving skills, **iv** .... techniques, mindfulness training and diversion techniques.

> coping   real world   rehearsal   relaxation

c Application and follow-through: this is the time for clients to **i** .... what they have learned in the **ii** .... , with increasingly more stressful situations. In order to build up to this, techniques may be used, such as **iii** .... a stressful situation or role-playing.

> apply   real world   visualising

KEY WORD

stress inoculation training (SIT): a type of cognitive–behavioural therapy designed to expose people to increasing levels of stress to develop coping skills. There are three phases: conceptualisation, skills acquisition and rehearsal, and application and follow-through

2   Complete the following sentences to evaluate SIT.

   a   SIT can be a very effective way of dealing with stress because ....

   b   SIT puts the individual in a position where they are able to ....

   c   A disadvantage of SIT is that it requires ....

   d   SIT does not work for everyone, as it relies on ....

8.5 Health promotion

Exercise 13 Strategies for promoting health

This activity will allow you to check your knowledge and understanding of research into strategies for promoting health.

Anya and Willow are discussing the best strategies for promoting health. Anya suggests it would be best to scare people into making healthy choices. Willow argues that a better approach would be to inform people so that they can make informed decisions for themselves.

1   To what extent do you agree with Anya? Use a study to help with your answer.

2   To what extent do you agree with Willow? Use a study to help with your answer.

Exercise 14 Health promotion in schools and worksites

This activity will allow you to check your knowledge and understanding of research into promoting healthy eating in schools.

1   Analyse how rewards and peer modelling could work to promote healthy eating in schools. Use a study of your choice to help you.

2   Give **two** reasons why a healthy eating intervention might work to increase healthy eating in schools.

Exercise 15 Individual factors in changing health beliefs

KEY WORD

positive psychology: the scientific study of the three different happy lives: the Pleasant Life, the Good Life and the Meaningful Life.

This exercise will allow you to check your understanding of positive psychology and the study by Shoshani and Steinmetz (2014), and to apply your knowledge.

1   For each of the following outlines, which **positive psychology** 'life' is being most accurately described?

   a   Yin lives a busy life, but he always finds time to volunteer at the local animal rescue centre and donate food to the homeless.

   b   Parminder is proud to work as a nurse, and volunteers by helping at the hospital in her spare time too.

   c   Lydia likes to have long, hot baths. She also enjoys having dinner with her friends.

2   Answer the following questions about the key study by Shoshani and Steinmetz (2014).

   a   How many students were in the sample?

   b   What country was the study carried out in?

   c   What questionnaire was used to measure the students' mental health?

   d   How were the teachers trained in the intervention programme?

   e   What were two main risk factors for students' mental health?

RESEARCH METHODS

This exercise will allow you to apply your understanding of research methods. It will also enable you to design a study.

1   Define the following terms:

   a   Independent variable

   b   Dependent variable

   c   Closed question

   d   Open question

2   Design a study to compare the effectiveness of stimulation therapy/TENS in pain management for patients with chronic pain, compared to using standard painkillers only.

   You should consider:

   •   the independent and dependent variable(s)

   •   two variables you can control

   •   the sample

   •   a self-report method with an example of a question.

3   a   Describe **one** strength and **one** weakness of the study you have designed.

   b   Describe **one** way the study would be stronger and **one** way it would be weaker if you used a case study instead.

ISSUES AND DEBATES

This exercise will help you to check your understanding of the free will versus determinism debate and to consider how it relates to health psychology.

1 State whether each of the following statements applies to free will or determinism.

   a We are responsible for our own decisions.

   b Behaviour results from internal factors, such as genes and hormones.

   c Things that happen to you will affect how you behave.

   d You make your own choices in life.

   e The biological and behavioural approach relate to this side of the debate.

2 Describe **one** source of stress and explain why it is deterministic.

3 Give **one** strength and **one** weakness of a deterministic approach to sources of stress.

Chapter 9

Organisational psychology

LEARNING INTENTIONS

In this chapter you will practise how to:

- describe and evaluate theory and research into motivation to work in terms of needs theories, cognitive theories and motivators at work

- describe and evaluate theory and research into leadership and management in terms of traditional and modern theories of leadership, leadership styles, leaders and followers

- describe and evaluate theory and research into group behaviour in organisations in terms of group development and decision-making, individual and group performance and conflict at work

- describe and evaluate theory and research into organisational work conditions in terms of physical work conditions, temporal conditions and health and safety

- describe and evaluate theory and research into satisfaction at work in terms of theories of job satisfaction, measuring job satisfaction and attitudes to work.

9.1 Motivation to work

Exercise 1 Need theories

KEY WORD

validity: the extent to which the researcher is testing what they claim to be testing

This exercise will allow you to demonstrate your ability to describe and evaluate projective tests as a methodology.

1   Describe what is meant by a 'projective test'.

2   Evaluate **one** strength and **one** weakness of using projective tests. Use examples from organisational psychology to support your answer.

Exercise 2 Cognitive theories

This exercise will allow you to demonstrate your ability to describe Latham and Locke's goal-setting theory in detail.

1   Identify, describe and give an example of SMART goals that can be used by a student working towards a qualification. Parts of the table have been completed to get you started.

Principle	Description	Example
Specific	*Being particular rather than general.*	a
b	c	*To achieve 60 per cent or more on my homework and practice assessments.*
d	*Being realistic about what can be achieved.*	e
f	g	*To be able to progress to the next level of my qualification.*
Timescale	h	i

Exercise 3 Motivators at work

KEY WORDS
intrinsic: something that comes from within; internal
extrinsic: something that comes from the outside; external

This exercise will allow you to demonstrate your ability to describe Deci and Ryan's self-determination theory in detail.

1   Match each aspect of self-determination theory to its correct description.

Aspect		Description	
a	competence	i	having the freedom to make choices
b	autonomy	ii	possessing the knowledge or skills to achieve a goal
c	relatedness	iii	a feeling of belonging to a group

2   Explain whether self-determination theory is based on '**intrinsic**' or '**extrinsic**' motivation.

9.2 Leadership and management

Exercise 4 Leadership style

This exercise will allow you to apply Muczyk and Reimann's theory of leader behaviour to the real world.

You have recently been appointed leader of a group activity conducting a research project with your peers. All the team members are very experienced in this area of work, and eager to help direct the project as they have managed the work well for some time without a leader.

1   State the style of leadership behaviour you would choose to use in this scenario.

2   Suggest **one** benefit of the style of leadership you have chosen.

3   Suggest **one** limitation of the style of leadership you have chosen.

Exercise 5 Leadership style and gender

KEY WORDS

autocratic leadership: behaviour style in which the leader controls all the decisions with little to no input from group members

democratic leadership: behaviour style in which the leader shares decision-making with group members

This exercise will allow you to demonstrate your ability to apply the findings of Cuadrado et al.'s (2008) study to real-life.

Li has attended a training workshop on leadership styles. She is considering how she can use a more **democratic leadership** style with her own team. Li's colleague is concerned that using this style of leadership may mean that Li is not taken seriously as a manager as the leader of their organisation is a man.

1   State the style of leadership which is considered stereotypically masculine.

2   Suggest whether Li will be disadvantaged if she uses a democratic leadership style with her team, using findings from the study by Cuadrado et al. to support your answer.

Exercise 6 Leaders and followers

This exercise will allow you to demonstrate your ability to describe Kelley's (1988) five styles of followers.

Yasmin is part of a team carrying out a project to design a new piece of software. Yasmin thinks her manager's plan for the project does not give the team enough time to complete the software design.

1   Name the two dimensions of followers and non-followers identified by Kelley.

2   Suggest how Yasmin might behave as a follower if she was:

   a   a sheep

   b   a pragmatic

   c   a star follower

> **TIP**
>
> When applying your knowledge of a study, you might need to make use of specific results to support your answer. Results mean reporting the data that was collected in the study.

9.3 Group behaviour in organisations

Exercise 7 Group development and decision-making

> **KEY WORD**
>
> **cognitive bias:** systematic errors in thinking that happen when people are interpreting information

Faulty decision-making is an area of concern for many organisations. This exercise will allow you to demonstrate your ability to describe this topic.

Forsyth (2006) suggests that there are three categories of potential biases that may affect group decision-making.

1   State the three causes or 'sins' identified by Forsyth.

2   An organisation has spent lots of money on developing a product that is now unlikely to sell well. The team in charge of development decides to continue with development anyway.

   Suggest which sub-type of biased decision the team in this scenario is making.

Exercise 8 Individual and group performance

This exercise will allow you to demonstrate your ability to evaluate Claypoole and Szalma's (2019) study in terms of methodology.

1   Complete the paragraph about the strengths and weaknesses of Claypoole and Szalma's methodology. Fill in the gaps using words from the box.

This key study lacks **a** .... as it took place in an artificial

environment. Participants in a field study under realistic conditions might have

different **b** .... rates or response times. However, the study

had high **c** .... due to using a **d** ....

procedure with set timings for the display of stimuli such as the critical signals

or the **e** .... of the EPM equipment.

| detection   ecological validity   positioning   **reliability**   standardised |

2   Suggest why the sample used by the researchers may be difficult to generalise from.

Exercise 9 Conflict at work

This exercise will allow you to apply the topic of bullying at work to the real world.

Willow has experienced repeated verbal abuse from his colleague.

1   State the **two** causes of **bullying**.

2   Suggest how each cause could explain Willow's bullying.

9.4 Organisational work conditions

Exercise 10 Temporal conditions of work environments

<table>
<tr><td>KEY WORD</td></tr>
<tr><td>temporal conditions: relating to time and how working patterns are arranged</td></tr>
</table>

This exercise will allow you to demonstrate your ability to describe the different forms of working patterns.

1   Match each **temporal condition** to its correct description.

Temporal condition		Description	
a	shift work	i	employees with working hours that are arranged around agreed core times
b	on-call	ii	employees who do not have the same work pattern every week
c	flexi-time	iii	employees who are on stand-by to begin work, often at short notice

2   Explain the difference between rapid rotation and slow rotation.

3   Which shift pattern is easier for workers to cope with?

Exercise 11 Health and safety

This exercise will allow you to demonstrate your ability to describe the two main theories that explain the cause of accidents at work.

1   Compare the similarities and differences between the human error approach and errors in operator–machine systems.

2   Give **one** example of an accident at work caused by errors in operator-machine systems.

3   Outline the role of a human factor expert.

Exercise 12 Reducing accidents at work

KEY WORD
token economy: a system in which people receive tokens (secondary reinforcers) for certain targeted behaviours. Tokens can then be exchanged for rewards (primary reinforcers)

This exercise will help you apply knowledge of reducing accidents at work to the real-world.

A large manufacturing organisation has a high turnover of staff. Existing staff are taking many days off as sick leave and reporting high levels of stress.

1   Define what is meant by 'absenteeism', using the scenario as an example.

2   Suggest how a **token economy**, as investigated by Fox et al. (1987), could be used to address the problems in the scenario.

3   Outline the ethical issues you might need to consider when using a token economy in the workplace.

9.5 Satisfaction at work

Exercise 13 Theories of job satisfaction

This exercise will help you demonstrate your ability to describe the range of techniques used to design or redesign jobs so as to improve employee satisfaction.

1   Define what is meant by 'job enrichment'.

2   Analyse how a leisure centre could use job rotation to improve employee satisfaction.

3   Analyse **one** of the reasons why it might be difficult to implement job enlargement in a workplace of your choice.

Exercise 14 Measuring job satisfaction

This exercise will allow you to apply Walton's quality of working life (QWL) typology to the real-world.

1   Amir works in human resources for a large organisation. He has been asked to consider how the organisation can improve the quality of working life for its employees.

For each of Walton's eight conditions, suggest how Amir could apply it in his organisation.

Condition	How to apply
a Fair and adequate payment	
b Safe and healthy working conditions	
c Providing opportunities to use and develop skills	
d Opportunity for career growth and security	
e Positive social relationships/integration within the workplace	
f The total life space	
g Constitutionalism (policies and procedures) in the workplace	
h Social relevance	

Exercise 15 Attitudes to work

KEY WORD

sabotage: in the workplace this includes any employee behaviour designed to cause a production or profit loss to the organisation

This exercise will allow you to demonstrate your ability to describe the results and conclusions of Giacalone and Rosenfeld's (1987) study.

1   State which group was more likely to justify production slowdowns.

2   State which group was more likely to justify dishonesty.

3   Outline **one** conclusion from Giacalone and Rosenfeld's study.

RESEARCH METHODS

This exercise will allow you to evaluate the use of field studies in organisational psychology.

1 Describe **one** strength of using field studies, using any example from organisational psychology.

2 Describe **one** weakness of using field studies, using any example from organisational psychology.

ISSUES AND DEBATES

This exercise will help you to consider the importance of the nature–nurture debate in organisational psychology.

1 Define what is meant by 'nature'.

2 Define what is meant by 'nurture'.

3 Copy and complete the table to show how the nature–nurture debate can be applied to explain leadership and management.

		Nature	Nurture
a	universalist theories	i	ii
b	adaptive leadership	i	ii
c	leadership practices inventory	i	ii

> Workbook glossary

abbreviation: a shortened form of a word of phrase; often using the first letters of the words involved.

adoption study: a type of study looking at the similarities between adopted individuals and their biological parents as a way of investigating the differing influences of biology and environment.

aggression: behaviour that is aimed at harming others either physically or psychologically.

amplitude: the 'height' of waves, e.g. on an EEG (indicating voltage).

arousal: the extent to which we are alert, for example responsive to external sensory stimuli. It has physiological and psychological components and is mediated by the nervous system and hormones.

authority: a person or organisation in a position of power who can give orders and requires obedience.

autocratic leadership: behaviour style in which the leader controls all the decisions with little to no input from group members.

autism spectrum disorder (ASD): a diagnostic category (previously including Autism and Asperger's syndrome). Symptoms, appearing in childhood, present a range of difficulties with social interaction and communication and restricted, repetitive or inflexible behaviours or interests.

Beck Depression Inventory (BDI): this is the world's most widely used measure of depression, where respondents are asked how much they agree with a range of statements.

blank slate: the idea that all individuals are born without any mental content, and that all knowledge must come from experience.

brand name: the name used by a company to distinguish their products or services from other companies' products or services. It is their key identity and cannot be easily changed.

bullying: a pattern of behaviour in which one or more people harm and/or embarrass others.

bystander apathy: when a bystander does not show concern for a person in need.

case study: a research method in which a single instance, e.g. one person, family or institution, is studied in detail.

ceiling effect: this occurs when a test is too easy and all participants in a condition achieve a very high score. This is problematic as it does not allow the researcher to differentiate between results.

circadian rhythm: a cycle that repeats daily, i.e. approximately every 24 hours, such as the sleep/wake cycle.

classical conditioning: learning through association, studied in both humans and animals.

cognitive bias: systematic errors in thinking that happen when people are interpreting information.

cognitive dissonance: the feeling of discomfort that comes from holding two conflicting beliefs, or when there is a conflict between beliefs and behaviours.

community interventions: any attempts to encourage a certain behaviour in a town or city, using methods such as leafleting, letters and lotteries.

controls: ways to keep potential confounding variables constant, e.g. between levels of the independent variable, to ensure measured differences in the dependent variable are likely to be due to the independent variable, raising validity.

correlation coefficient: a number between −1 and 1 which shows the strength of a relationship between two variables, with a coefficient of −1 meaning there is a perfect negative correlation and a coefficient of 1 meaning there is a perfect positive correlation.

counterconditioning: replacing a conditioned response, such as fear, with another response, such as a feeling of calm.

democratic leadership: behaviour style in which the leader shares decision-making with group members.

dependent variable: the factor in an experiment that is measured and is expected to change under the influence of the independent variable.

differential effect: when one or more individuals experience a difference in outcome when exposed to the same stimuli.

diffusion of responsibility: when there are other people available to help in an emergency, an individual may be less likely to take action because they feel a reduced sense of personal responsibility.

dream: a vivid, visual sequence of imagery that occurs at regular intervals during sleep and is associated with rapid eye movements.

dual task situation: an experimental set-up that includes simultaneous cognitive demands of a primary task and a concurrent task.

duration: the length of time something lasts, for example how long symptoms have been present.

electroencephalograph (EEG): a machine used to detect and record electrical activity in the brain and muscles when many cells are active at the same time. It uses macroelectrodes, which are large electrodes stuck to the skin or scalp.

ethical guidelines: pieces of advice that guide psychologists to consider the welfare of participants and wider society.

ethical issues: problems in research that raise concerns about the welfare of participants (or have the potential for a wider negative impact on society).

experimental design: the way in which participants are allocated to levels of the independent variable.

extrinsic: something that comes from the outside; external.

family study: a type of study investigating whether biological relatives of those with a disorder are more likely than non-biological relatives to be similarly affected.

field experiment: an investigation looking for a causal relationship in which an independent variable is manipulated and is expected to be responsible for changes in the dependent variable. It is conducted in the normal environment for the participants for the behaviour being investigated and some control of variables is possible.

filler questions: items put into a questionnaire, interview or test to disguise the aim of the study by hiding the important questions among irrelevant ones so that participants are less likely to work out the aims and then alter their behaviour.

frequency: the number of events per fixed period of time, e.g. the number of eye movements per minute (approximately 60/minute in REM sleep) or the number of brain waves (cycles) per second, or Hertz (Hz), e.g. 13–30 Hz for beta waves.

gender stereotype: a bias exhibited in society, which may be held by people and represented, for example, in books or toys that assign particular traits, behaviours, emotions, occupations, etc., to males and females.

generalisability: how widely findings apply, e.g. to other settings and populations.

habituated: when a person becomes accustomed to something. When someone is frequently exposed to a certain stimulus then over time, they become used to it.

heuristics: mental shortcuts that can help us when making decisions but can lead to errors in judgement.

ICD-11: the 11th edition of the International Classification of Diseases. This is the global standard for coding health information and includes both physical and mental health disorders. It was developed and is updated by the World Health Organisation (WHO).

imagery exposure therapy: therapy in which the person is asked to vividly imagine their feared object, situation or activity.

independent measures: an experimetal design in which a different group of participants is used for each level of the independent variable (condition).

independent variable: the factor under investigation in an experiment that is manipulated to create two or more conditions (levels) and is expected to be responsible for changes in the dependent variable.

individual-situational debate: this is the debate about the relative influence or interaction of a person's unique physiology or personality (individual) and factors in the environment (situational) on thinking and behaviour.

informed consent: knowing enough about a study to decide whether you want to agree to participate.

inhibit: to hinder or prevent. In neuropsychology, inhibition occurs when a chemical or chemical process is reduced or stopped.

input: how we take incoming information in, for example eyes (detecting light, colour and movement), ears (detecting sound), skin (detecting pressure).

interview: a research method using verbal questions asked directly, using techniques such as face-to-face or telephone.

intrinsic: something that comes from within; internal.

life events: any major changes in your life (either positive or negative). The key aspect of a life event is that it requires some aspect of transition in your life.

Likert-type scale: a type of question used in surveys and questionnaires, where the respondent is asked to answer on a scale of, for example 1–7, the extent to which they agree with a range of statements.

localisation of function: the way that particular brain areas are responsible for different activities

logo: a symbol used by a company to act as a visual cue to allow faster processing and universal brand recognition across languages and cultures.

mean: the measure of central tendency calculated by adding up the values of all the scores and dividing by the number of scores in the data set.

measure of central tendency: a mathematical way to find the typical or average score from a data set, using the mode, median or mean.

measure of spread: a mathematical way to describe the variation or dispersion within a data set.

meta-analysis: data from a range of studies into the same subject is combined and analysed to get an overall understanding of the trends.

mindfulness: a state achieved through meditation which aims to increase awareness of the present-moment experience and enable a person to look at themselves in a compassonate, non-judgemental way.

model: person who inspires or encourages others to imitate positive or negative behaviours.

musculoskeletal: referring to the muscles, bones, ligaments and tendons in the body.

nature: innate, genetic factors which influence behaviour.

non-rapid eye movement (nREM) sleep: the stages of sleep (1 to 4) in which our eyes are still. It is also called quiescent (quiet) sleep. It is not associated with dreaming.

nurture: environmental influences on behaviour.

objectivity: the impact of an unbiased external viewpoint on, for example, how data is interpreted. Interpretation is not affected by an individual's feelings, beliefs or experiences, so should be consistent between different researchers.

oestrogen: a hormone released mainly by the ovaries, so is considered to be a 'female' hormone.

operant conditioning: learning through the consequences of our actions.

operational definition: the clear description of a variable such that it can be accurately manipulated, measured or quantified, and the study can be replicated. This includes the way that the independent variable and dependant variable in experiments and the co-variables in correlations are described.

operationalisation: the clear definition or description of a variable so that it can be accurately manipulated, measured or quantified, and the study can be replicated. This includes the independent variable and dependent variable in experiments and the co-variables in correlations.

output: how we send information out, for example voice, body (such as hands for writing, drawing, moving).

oxytocin: a social hormone found in humans that heightens the importance of social cues and is linked to positive social behaviours like helping others.

personal space: the physical space around someone, which they consider to be psychologically theirs.

phobia: the irrational, persistent fear of an object or event (stimulus) that poses little real danger but creates anxiety and avoidance in the sufferer.

play: behaviour typical of childhood that appears to be done for fun rather than any useful purpose. It may be solitary or social and may or may not involve interaction with an object. Objects designed for the purpose of play are called 'toys'.

pleasure-arousal-dominance (PAD) model: a model designed to demonstrate how physical environments influence people through emotional impact: pleasure, arousal and dominance.

positive psychology: the scientific study of the three different happy lives: the Pleasant Life, the Good Life and the Meaningful Life.

positive reinforcement: when a behaviour results in a reward, such as money or attention, that behaviour is likely to be repeated again.

processing: how information is dealt with, for example thinking and decision-making in the brain, brain functions such as short-term and long-term memory.

prostaglandins: hormone-like substances that cause pain.

protection from harm: participants should not be exposed to any greater physical or psychological risk than they would expect in their day-to-day life.

qualitative data: descriptive, in-depth results indicating the quality of a psychological characteristic, such as responses to open questions in self-reports or case studies and detailed observations.

quantitative data: numerical results about the amount or quantity of a psychological measure, such as pulse rate or a score on an intelligence test.

questionnaire: a self-report research method that uses written questions, through a 'paper and pencil' or online technique.

rapid eye movement (REM) sleep: a stage of sleep in which our eyes move rapidly under the lids, which is associated with vivid, visual dreams.

reliability: the extent to which a procedure, task or measure is consistent, for example, that it would produce the same results with the same people on each occasion.

right to withdraw: a participant should know they can remove themselves, and their data, from a study at any time.

sabotage: in the workplace this includes any employee behaviour designed to cause a production or profit loss to the organisation.

sample: the group of people selected to represent the population in a study.

secondary positive reinforcement: training in which a secondary reinforcer such as a sound marker is used and then followed with administration of a primary positive reinforcer (typically food).

severity: the extent of something, or how bad it is. For example, symptoms may be mild, moderate or severe.

sleep: a state of reduced conscious awareness and reduce movement that occurs on a daily cycle.

slogan: a short memorable phrase used in advertising a product.

social cues: these are facial expressions or body language which people use to send messages to one another, for example a smile to indicate happiness.

social desirability bias: trying to present oneself in the best light by determining what a task requires.

socialisation: the process of learning to behave in socially acceptable ways. This may differ somewhat for the two genders and in different cultures.

social learning theory: the learning of a new behaviour that is observed in a role model and imitated later in the absence of that mode.

social readjustment rating scale (SSRS): a scale consisting of 43 life events; the respondent must identify any of the events they have experienced during a period of time. Each life event is given a score in terms of life change units (LCUs) and a total score is used to predict likelihood of stress-related illness.

social salience: the importance or attention someone gives to cues from other people, e.g. body language, interpersonal distance and expressions.

stimulus: an event or object that leads to a behavioural response.

stoicism: a philosophy where one of the principles is that the individual is not directly affected by outside things but by their own perception of external things.

stress inoculation training (SIT): a type of cognitive-behavioural therapy designed to expose people to increasing levels of stress to develop coping skills. There are three phases: conceptualisation, skills acquisition and rehearsal, and application and follow-through.

subjectivity: the effect of an individual's personal viewpoint on, for example, how they interpret data. Interpretation can differ between individual researchers as a viewpoint may be biased by one's feelings, beliefs or experiences, so is not independent of the situation.

temporal conditions: relating to time and how working patterns are arranged.

testosterone: a hormone released mainly by the testes, so is considered to be a 'male' hormone. It is an example of an androgen.

token economy: a reward system used, where tokens are given for specific desirable behaviour and these tokens can then be exchanged for goods

twin study: a type of study that compares sets of twins to analyse similarities and differences. This may include concordance for intelligence or mental disorders. Both monozygotic (MZ) and dizygotic (DZ) twins are studied, and their concordance rate is compared.

ultradian rhythm: a cycle that repeats more often than daily, e.g. the occurrence of periods of dreaming every 90 minutes during sleep.

validity: the extent to which the researcher is testing what they claim to be testing.